Gaz Oakley

Plants Only Holidays

Indulgent, Plant-Forward Recipes
for the Festive Season

Photography by Simon Smith & Tom Kong

quadrille

Introduction

The Christmas period, for me, is the season of warmth and joy
that brings people together. In the darkest, coldest months
of the year, when my garden is in hibernation – and even I feel
like going into a long winter snooze – the Christmas spirit
is one that fills me with a sense of excitement.

Christmas means meeting up with old friends, creating
memories, sharing love and, most importantly, gathering
around the dining table to share a lot of food!

With *Plants Only Holidays*, I've embarked on a journey to
reimagine party food, Christmas dinner, and all the trimmings
that go along with it.

Cooking with just plants doesn't need to be restrictive, boring
or unimaginative. For me, cooking with plants is peaceful
cuisine, during one the most peaceful times of the year, and
I think our dinner tables should reflect that too. But don't
worry, with these recipes you won't be missing out on any of
the indulgence – and I promise there's something here that even
the biggest meat eater will enjoy.

Each Christmas, I come up with new exciting recipes to fill the
dinner table, so that's why I've remade this Christmas book, adding
in a load of new recipes and updating some of the original ones.

Thank you for being on this journey with me,
and happy holidays!

Ingredients and equipment

Agar agar powder or flakes are a sea-vegetable gelling agent – so basically a vegan gelatine. It's brilliant stuff and can contribute to some amazing dishes!

Agave nectar is the sweet nectar extracted from several species of the agave plant, the majority of which are grown in Mexico or South Africa. It is a great natural sweetener. In my recipes, I tend to advise using either agave nectar or maple syrup, as they are very similar in terms of sweetness; however, agave is often slightly more affordable.

Liquid smoke This handy little flavouring is an optional ingredient in my recipes, but it's absolutely great at creating a smoky flavour.

Miso paste Made from fermented soy beans, this paste has a super-strong umami flavour. You can find it in the Asian section of most supermarkets. It's a staple ingredient in Japanese cooking. Soy-free miso pastes can also be found and are made from rice and legumes. Alternatively, you can replace it with things like tomato purée (paste), coconut aminos or Marmite.

Nori is made by shredding edible seaweed and then pressing it into thin sheets. It's often used when making sushi. I often use it to achieve a "taste-of-the-sea" flavour.

Nutritional yeast is a deactivated yeast. It has a strong flavour that is quite nutty, cheesy and creamy, which makes it the perfect ingredient in my vegan "cheese" recipes and lots of other recipes where I need a bold flavour.

Vital wheat gluten This is an ingredient made from gluten – the main protein of wheat. This product has been used in vegetarian recipes for years (Buddhist monks used it as a meat replacement) and it's often used in Asian cookery. I have modernized many ancient recipes to produce some stunning dishes. Meat replacements aren't for everyone, and the shop-bought replacements are highly processed; at least when making your own, you can see every ingredient that goes in. It can be purchased from good health food stores or online in powder form.

Tapioca starch Tapioca is extracted from the cassava root. This magic starch gives my homemade "cheeses" a great stringy, cheese-like texture.

Tofu is the first plant-based protein people think of. I have some incredible ways to turn this subtle-flavoured ingredient into something spectacular. Also known as beancurd, it is cultivated by coagulating soy milk and then pressing the resulting curds into soft, white blocks. Tofu can be soft, firm, or extra firm. I use firm tofu in all the recipes in my book.

Cooking times When I refer to cooking times, these are to give a general impression of how long each dish takes from start to finish – but everyone cooks at different speeds, and these are only guidelines.

Powerful blender One of the most important pieces of equipment in a good vegan kitchen is a powerful blender and lots of my recipes rely on one. I promise that it will be a really good investment! I recommend a Ninja Kitchen System.

Christmas Morning

Earl Grey, Chestnut and Cranberry Cinnamon Rolls

I'm yet to meet a single person who doesn't like cinnamon rolls, and this festive version is packed with cranberry and chestnuts.

For the dough

400g (3⅓ cups) strong white bread flour, plus extra for dusting

60g (½ cup) icing (confectioner's) sugar

2 tsp fast action dried yeast

250ml (1 cup) Earl Grey tea, lukewarm

180ml (¾ cup) non-dairy milk, lukewarm

5 tbsp olive oil, plus extra for greasing

For the filling

1 x 180g (6¼oz) pouch vacuum-packed whole cooked chestnuts, finely chopped

85g (½ cup) dried cranberries, chopped

3 tbsp ground cinnamon

5 tbsp light brown sugar

110g (½ cup) plant butter, melted

For the icing

90g (⅔ cup) icing (confectioner's) sugar

100g (scant ½ cup) plant-based cream cheese

55g (¼ cup) plant butter

2 tsp vanilla extract or vanilla bean paste

Makes

9

Cooks In

60 minutes

+ rising time

Difficulty

5/10

First, prepare the dough. Add all the dry ingredients to your stand mixer (with a dough hook attached) or to a mixing bowl. Mix together, then add the wet ingredients. Bring the mix together into a ball, then knead on medium speed for 5–6 minutes (or about 8 minutes by hand). Once you've kneaded the dough, lightly grease a large mixing bowl and place the dough in. Cover the bowl with a wet tea (dish) towel and place it somewhere warm for around 90 minutes, or until the dough has doubled in size. Alternatively, place the dough in the fridge overnight to slowly rise, saving you time making the rolls the next day. While the dough proves, mix together the filling ingredients in a small mixing bowl.

Lightly flour your surface and turn the risen dough out of the bowl. Roll the dough into a rectangle measuring roughly 25 x 50cm (10 x 20in) around 1cm (½in) thick. Spread the filling mixture over the rolled out dough,

leaving a 2.5cm (1in) border bare around the edges. Roll the dough up from a long side into a long sausage shape, quite tight if you can, then cut the sausage into 9 slices. Arrange the slices, cut sides up, in a lightly greased baking dish/tray, then cover with a clean tea towel and place somewhere warm for around 45 minutes for them to rise.

Preheat your oven to 180ºC (350ºF). Once the rolls have risen, place them into the oven on the bottom shelf. Bake the rolls for 35 minutes until beautiful and golden.

Meanwhile whisk together the icing ingredients.

Remove the buns from the oven and let them cool for 15 minutes in the dish with a tea towel over the top – this will ensure your rolls stay nice and soft.

Top the rolls with lashings of icing before serving.

Winter Veg Hash Browns and Beans

These hash browns showcase how versatile winter root veggies are, and I'll often make them with whatever root veg I have in excess. Served with hearty beans, they are the perfect winter breakfast.

2 large Maris Piper potatoes, peeled
200g (1 cup) grated winter root vegetables, such as parsnip, swede (rutabaga), carrot, celeriac (celery root)
1 tsp sea salt
½ tsp black pepper
handful of parsley, chopped
4 spring onions (scallions), finely chopped
2 tbsp plain (all-purpose) flour
2 tbsp chia seeds or sesame seeds
3 tbsp olive oil, plus extra for frying

For the proper beans
1 onion, finely chopped
1 tbsp olive oil
1 tsp garlic granules
1 tsp smoked paprika

1 tbsp dried sage
1 tbsp tomato purée (paste)
2 tbsp maple syrup
2 tbsp soy sauce
1 tbsp white wine vinegar
200g (1 cup) cooked butter beans (from a can or jar is best)
200g (1 cup) cooked haricot beans (from a can or jar is best)
1 x 400g (14oz) can of chopped tomatoes
sea salt and pepper

To serve
greens
sautéed mushrooms
red cabbage sauerkraut, optional (page 177)
mixed seeds

Serves
4

Cooks In
30 minutes

Difficulty
3/10

Can be gluten-free

Preheat your oven to 180ºC (350ºF) and line a large baking tray with greaseproof paper.

Lay a clean tea (dish) towel out flat on your work surface. Grate the potatoes and root vegetables into the centre of the towel, then pick up the corners and ring out all the liquid into your sink.

Transfer the mixture to a large mixing bowl and add the salt, pepper, parsley, spring onions, flour, seeds and olive oil. Mix together really well, then form into patties around 2cm (¾in) thick and 6cm (2½in) in diameter. Place the patties onto the prepared baking tray.

Preheat a large non-stick frying pan over a medium heat and, when the pan is hot, add a little olive oil. Cook the hash-browns for 3–4 minutes on each side, making sure

that they go golden and crisp. Place the hash browns back onto the baking tray, then into the oven to finish cooking for 15 minutes.

Meanwhile, to make the beans, sauté the onion in the olive oil in a small saucepan. When it's golden, add the garlic granules, smoked paprika and sage, and season with salt and pepper. Stir through the tomato purée, maple syrup, soy sauce and vinegar. Turn the heat down low and add the beans, stirring well to make sure everything is well coated. Add the chopped tomatoes, pop a lid on the pan and let the beans bubble away for 10 minutes.

To serve, stack your hash browns and serve with greens, sautéed mushrooms, red cabbage sauerkraut (if using), a sprinkle of mixed seeds and, of course, plenty of beans.

CHRISTMAS MORNING

Caramelized Bananas

Banana and peanut butter are a match made in heaven.
Even better when you caramelize the banana! This is a perfect
start to Christmas Day – and also very quick and simple to make!

1 tbsp coconut oil
3 bananas, cut into slices,
    at an angle
2 tbsp coconut sugar
2 tbsp peanut butter
2 slices of toast (or gluten-free
    bread)

To serve
fresh mint leaves
zest of 1 lime
handful of walnuts
handful of blueberries
handful of coconut flakes
1 tbsp maple syrup

Serves
2

Cooks In
25 minutes

Difficulty
2/10

**Can be GF,
if GF bread
is used**

Place a heavy-based non-stick frying pan over a medium heat. Add the coconut oil, wait for it to melt, then add the banana slices. Fry for 3 minutes on each side, until they're nicely caramelized. Sprinkle over the coconut sugar while they are cooking.

Spread the peanut butter generously onto the two slices of toast and top with the caramelized bananas.

Divide the toppings between the two, finishing with a drizzle of maple syrup.

Tofu Benedict

Wow your guests with this beautiful breakfast,
it's a real show stopper. The "hollandaise" is velvety
and smooth, the perfect match for smoky tofu.

225g (8oz) block firm smoked tofu,
    pressed to remove water
2 tbsp olive oil, for frying
pinch of black salt (optional for an
    "eggy" flavour, or use sea salt)
pinch of ground pepper

For the "hollandaise" sauce
120ml (½ cup) soy milk
3 tbsp white wine vinegar
½ tsp English mustard
pinch of sea salt and pepper
120ml (½ cup) olive oil

For the sautéed spinach
4 big handfuls of baby spinach
pinch of sea salt and pepper

To serve
2 breakfast muffins or bagels
handful of cherry tomatoes, halved
small bunch of fresh chives, finely chopped
pinch of cress

Serves
2

Cooks In
25 minutes

Difficulty
2/10

**Can be GF, if GF
bread is used**

First up, make the "hollandaise" sauce. Pour the soy milk, vinegar, mustard and seasoning into a measuring jug and blend using an electric stick blender, until mixed well. Keep the blender running and slowly trickle in the oil until the sauce starts to thicken up. Once you've added all the oil it should be thick and creamy but still pourable. If your sauce is too thick, stir in a few additional tablespoons of soy milk. Taste to check the seasoning. Cover the sauce with cling film (plastic wrap) and refrigerate until you're ready to serve.

Cut the tofu into rounds using an 8cm (3in) cutter. Pat dry with kitchen paper, then preheat a non-stick frying pan over a medium heat. Add the oil to the pan. Pan fry the tofu until golden on each side, around 3–4 minutes. Season with the black salt, if using, and pepper.

Remove the tofu from the pan and set aside. Turn the heat up high and add a touch more oil. When it starts to smoke add all the spinach (don't worry, it will wilt down quickly). Cook the spinach for 1 minute, stirring quickly. Season with a pinch of salt and pepper, then remove from the heat. Spinach contains lots of water, so I always press it with a clean tea (dish) towel to soak up any excess liquid.

Toast the muffins or bagels, if you like, then add the tofu slices and sautéed spinach. Scatter around the cherry tomato halves. Top with a dollop of the "hollandaise" sauce, sprinkle over some chopped chives, top with a pinch of cress and serve immediately.

CHRISTMAS MORNING

Sweet Potato Waffles with Sautéed Mushrooms

Cook the potato the day before to speed up the process on Christmas Day. Light and savoury – these make a great sharing breakfast.

For the waffles
2 tbsp chia seeds
160g (5½oz) cooked sweet potato
120g (1 cup) buckwheat flour
45g (½ cup) chickpea (gram) flour
360ml (1½ cups) non-dairy milk
2 tsp baking powder
1 tsp onion salt
2 tbsp maple syrup
¼ tsp cayenne pepper
handful of fresh chives
oil, for greasing

For the mushrooms
2 tbsp olive oil
300g (10½oz) mushrooms of your choice, halved
handful of cherry tomatoes
handful of chopped fresh parsley
pinch of sea salt and pepper

To serve
1 avocado, peeled and sliced
3 tbsp mixed seeds

Serves
2

Cooks In
45 minutes

Difficulty
5/10

GF

Measure the waffle ingredients into a blender and blend on a medium speed until fully combined. You may need to stop, scrape the sides and stir the mixture a couple of times. It should be the consistency of a thick pancake batter. If it is too thin, add a little more flour.

Preheat a waffle pan or machine to a medium temperature and lightly grease with oil. If your machine or pan is too hot, the middle of the waffle won't cook. When your waffle pan has reached temperature, pour in the batter (use a ladle) and leave the waffle pan to work its magic for 10–12 minutes. Cooking times may vary depending on your type of waffle pan or machine. Once your waffles are golden brown and quite firm to the touch, they are cooked – remove and keep warm in a preheated oven (150°C/300°F). Lightly grease the pan/machine before repeating with the remainder of the batter.

While the waffles are cooking, heat a non-stick frying pan over a low heat and add the olive oil. Sauté the mushrooms for 4–5 minutes, tossing the pan regularly. Once they are golden, throw in the tomatoes, parsley and seasoning and cook for 2–3 minutes.

Once the mushrooms and all the waffles are cooked, serve immediately with some sliced avocado on the side. Sprinkle over the mixed seeds.

Party Food and Light Meals

Rainbow Vegetable Terrine

Layer upon layer of flavour, if you live in a warm climate, this vibrant, colourful terrine might just be the perfect starter for your festive dinner. It's finished off with a carrot-top pesto. Delicious.

2 red (bell) peppers
2 yellow (bell) peppers
2 medium beetroots (beets), peeled
1 onion, peeled
1 large courgette (zucchini)
1 large aubergine (eggplant)
5 tbsp olive oil
1 tbsp fresh thyme leaves
8 fresh sage leaves, finely chopped
500g (1lb 2oz) rainbow chard leaves
    or spinach
crusty bread, to serve

For the creamy filling
200g (1 cup) silken tofu
zest and juice of 1 lemon

2 tbsp capers
pinch of chilli flakes
2 tbsp chopped fresh dill
pinch of sea salt and pepper

For the carrot top pesto
handful of carrot tops
handful of basil
2 garlic cloves
5 tbsp nuts of your choice, or seeds
zest and juice of ½ lemon
1 tsp miso paste
5 tbsp nutritional yeast flakes
2 tsp sea salt
125ml (½ cup) extra virgin olive oil

Serves
6

Cooks In
90 minutes

Difficulty
7/10

First up prepare the peppers; we need to remove the skins. Turn your grill (broiler) to maximum temperature and place the whole peppers on a roasting tray, then place under the grill. Make sure the peppers are no more than 10cm (4in) away from the grill as they need to be really close in order that the skins blister and char. Flip the peppers over after 5 minutes or so when the skins have blistered all over and they are slightly blackened. Once they have charred on both sides, remove the peppers from the grill and place them in a bowl. Cover with a plate to trap in the steam (this will make removing the skins much easier) and set them aside for 20 minutes.

Meanwhile, preheat the oven to 200ºC (400ºF). Cut the beetroots, onion, courgette and aubergine into slices about ½cm (¼in) thick and place on baking trays. Put the beets on their own tray or they will stain everything else pink. Drizzle the olive oil over both trays. Season with salt and pepper and sprinkle over the fresh herbs. Place both trays in the oven, prioritizing the beetroot on the higher shelf, and roast the vegetables for 35 minutes.

While they are cooking, peel the skins off the peppers using the back of your knife. Place the skins, seeds and stems of the peppers in your compost, so you are just left with the de-skinned flesh.

Recipe continued overleaf

Rainbow vegetable terrine continued...

Next, whip up the creamy filling – this will help bind everything together. Add the silken tofu to a mixing bowl along with the lemon zest and juice, capers, chilli flakes, dill and seasoning. Whisk the mixture together until thick and creamy, then cover and place in the fridge until needed.

Steam or blanch your chard or spinach leaves until just cooked. Transfer them to a clean tea (dish) towel and pat the leaves to soak up any excess water. The benefit of steaming is that the leaves will not absorb too much liquid.

When the beetroots, aubergine and courgette are cooked, remove from the oven and allow to cool completely.

Meanwhile make the carrot top pesto. Add all the ingredients to a food processor and blitz until relatively smooth – I like a few chunks left.

When all the vegetables are cool, line a terrine or 450g (1lb) loaf tin with baking parchment or cling film (plastic wrap), allowing 5cm (2in) of overhang.

Start by pressing the chard or spinach leaves into the terrine, covering the base and all the sides and reserving a few leaves for the top. Then start layering up the vegetables, alternating between the different layers, starting with the aubergine, followed by the peppers, beetroot, onions, courgette and a layer of the creamy filling. Drizzle a little pesto in from time to time as you build up the layers. Once you have filled the terrine, add one final layer of chard or spinach, then use the overhanging baking paper or cling film to cover the top of the terrine. Place a few weights on top (this can be a couple of cans of chickpeas) then pop the terrine into the fridge to set overnight or for at least 5 hours.

Serve the terrine chilled and in slices, with crusty bread and the rest of the pesto.

PARTY FOOD & LIGHT MEALS

Carrot "Lox" with "Cream Cheese", Capers and Dill Canapés

Preparing the carrot this way surprisingly emulates smoked salmon, harnessing the taste-of-the-sea flavour of nori seaweed. A delicious canapé that'll please everyone.

For the smoked "salmon"
440ml (scant 2 cups) vegetable stock
1 tbsp miso paste
3 tbsp sweet smoked paprika
1 large sheet of nori
2 tbsp maple syrup
2 tbsp smoked sea salt (or regular sea salt)
juice of 1 lemon
5 large carrots, peeled

For the "cream cheese"
125g (½ cup) raw cashew nuts
2 tbsp lemon juice
pinch of sea salt and white pepper

1 tbsp nutritional yeast
110ml (½ cup) filtered water

To serve
6 slices of toasted rye bread (or a gluten-free bread), cut into small pieces for canapés
lemon slices
3 tbsp capers
small handful of fresh dill

Serves
6

Cooks In
20 minutes

Difficulty
2/10

Can be GF, if GF bread is used

Place all the smoked "salmon" ingredients except the carrots into a medium saucepan, bring to the boil, then lower to a simmer for 10 minutes to let the flavours infuse.

While the broth is cooking, use a peeler to slice the carrots into long ribbons and place them in a large heatproof bowl.

Pour the broth through a sieve directly over the carrots into the bowl. This will lightly cook them. When the broth has cooled, cover the bowl with cling film (plastic wrap) or place the mixture into sterilized jars. Refrigerate

for at least a day (or up to seven days). The broth acts as a marinade.

To make the "cream cheese", soak the nuts in boiling water for 15 minutes. Drain away the soaking water and tip the nuts into a blender cup with the rest of the ingredients. Simply blitz everything until smooth, then use straight away or store in the fridge for 3–4 days.

To serve, generously spread the "cream cheese" onto pieces of toasted bread, top with the smoked "salmon" (drained of marinade), then top with lemon, capers and dill.

King Oyster Mushroom "Scallop" Risotto with Dill Oil

King oyster mushrooms are very succulent and, when cooked in a taste-of-the-sea broth, can pass as scallops. I serve them with a simple risotto, seasoned with a little dill oil.

For the "scallops"
5 king oyster (trumpet) mushrooms
4 tbsp olive oil

For the broth
2 sheets of nori, torn up roughly
1 shallot, finely sliced
1 garlic clove, finely sliced
2 tbsp white miso paste
10g (½ cup) dried mushrooms (I use porcini)
sprig of fresh thyme
250ml (1 cup) white wine
500ml (2 cups) vegetable stock
½ lemon

For the basic risotto
4 tbsp olive oil
4 shallots, finely chopped

4 garlic cloves, minced
1 tsp sea salt
400g (2 cups) risotto rice
250ml (1 cup) white wine
1 litre (4 cups) hot vegetable stock, plus a little extra if needed
2 tbsp nutritional yeast (optional)
black pepper

For the dill oil
large handful of dill
125ml (½ cup) olive oil (or flavourless oil of your choice)
pinch of sea salt

To serve
fresh dill
lemon zest
capers

Serves	**4**
Cooks In	**75 minutes**
Difficulty	**5/10**
	GF

First up, the "scallops". Remove the tops from the king oyster mushrooms (save these for a stir fry, perhaps), wash the stems, then slice into 2.5cm (1in) discs.

Add all the broth ingredients to a medium saucepan, place the lid on and let the broth bubble away and infuse for 5 minutes before adding the mushroom discs. Poach the mushrooms in the broth for 10 minutes. Once cooked,

remove the mushrooms from the broth and let them steam dry. Strain the broth into a large jug.

To make the risotto, heat the olive oil in a large saucepan over a medium heat and sauté the shallots and garlic, along with ½ teaspoon of the salt, until softened. Stir often and make sure they don't burn.

Recipe continued overleaf

King oyster mushroom "scallop" risotto with dill oil continued...

Once the shallots are soft, turn the heat down to low, add the risotto rice and stir well, making sure the rice is coated. I like to let my rice lightly toast, as it adds a slightly more nutty flavour to the finished risotto.

Pour in the white wine and stir every now and then until it has all been absorbed into the rice.

Once the wine has been soaked up, add a ladleful of stock (or you can use the reserved mushroom cooking broth), stir well, and when this has been absorbed add another ladleful, repeating until you have used up all the stock – this will take about 20 minutes.

Meanwhile, to make the dill oil, simply blitz all the ingredients together in a high-speed blender. When smooth, pass it through a fine sieve. The oil will store for a few weeks in a sealed container in the fridge.

After 20 minutes, the rice should look almost creamy. Check the rice is cooked – if it isn't, add a splash more stock, and carry on cooking for a bit. Once the rice is tender, stir in the nutritional yeast, if using. Check the risotto is seasoned well. If not add an extra pinch of salt and pepper.

To finish the "scallops", place a non-stick frying pan over a medium heat and add the 4 tablespoons of olive oil. Sear your steam-dried mushrooms on both sides for 3–4 minutes or until golden.

Serve the "scallops" on top of the risotto, drizzled with a little dill oil, and scattered with fresh dill, lemon zest and capers.

Butternut-squash arancini filled with "mozzarella"

I love to turn risotto into arancini. I use the basic risotto recipe, but stir through roasted pumpkin when the rice has just cooked.

½ large butternut squash
1 tbsp olive oil, plus optional extra
    for the sage
1 recipe quantity of Basic risotto (page 31)
10 sun-blushed tomatoes, chopped
handful of chopped parsley
1 tbsp chopped preserved lemon (optional)
50g (½ cup) panko or gluten-free
    breadcrumbs
1 litre (4 cups) vegetable oil, if frying
10 fresh sage leaves
sea salt and pepper

For coating
100g (1 cup) chickpea (gram) flour
120g (2 cups) panko breadcrumbs

For the "mozzarella"
120g (½ cup) raw cashew nuts
120ml (½ cup) filtered cold water
120ml (½ cup) cold non-dairy milk
4 tbsp tapioca starch
2 tbsp nutritional yeast
¼ tsp dried onion powder
1 tsp white miso
1 tsp lemon juice
pinch of sea salt and white pepper
¼ tsp garlic powder

To serve
Cranberry and orange sauce (page 114)

Makes
8–10 large arancini

Cooks In
2 hours

Difficulty
5/10

**Can be GF, if GF
breadcrumbs
are used**

Roast the squash before making the risotto. Preheat the oven to 180°C (350°F), slice the butternut squash in half lengthways and scoop out the seeds. Rub the cut surface with the olive oil and place cut-side down on a baking sheet. Roast for 1 hour until soft. When the squash is roasted, remove from the oven and leave to cool. Scoop out the flesh into a bowl.

Make the risotto following the recipe on pages 31–32, and once the rice is cooked, stir in the roasted butternut squash. Line a large baking tray with greaseproof paper and spread the risotto out over the tray. Leave it to cool for 30 minutes before chilling in the fridge for at least 2 hours.

While the risotto is cooling, make your "mozzarella". To quick soak the nuts: simply pop them in a heatproof container and pour over boiling water. Leave for around 20 minutes to soak while you measure out the other ingredients.

Once the nuts have softened, drain and add them to a high-speed blender with all the other "mozzarella" ingredients. Blend on full speed until you have a smooth mixture. I know it doesn't look anything like mozzarella now but bear with it!

Recipe continued overleaf

Butternut-squash arancini filled with "mozzarella" continued...

Scrape the mixture into a non-stick saucepan, arm yourself with a spatula and start stirring over a medium heat. Be patient – you will be stirring for around 8–10 minutes. Stir until it is super-thick and starts to come away from the sides of the saucepan, then remove from the heat and scrape the mixture into a sandwich bag. Set aside until you're ready to fill your arancini.

Once the rice is thoroughly chilled, scrape it into a mixing bowl and add the chopped sun-blush tomatoes, parsley, preserved lemon (if using) and the breadcrumbs. Mix carefully until incorporated, then divide the risotto mixture into approximately 100g (3½oz) balls. I like to make evenly sized balls, so grab your scales.

Cut a corner off a plastic sandwich bag to create a mini piping bag, so you can squeeze out the "mozzarella".

Lightly wet your hands (to stop the rice from sticking), then poke your thumb into the middle of each rice ball and squeeze in around two teaspoons of "mozzarella". Mould the rice mixture around the mozzarella to seal it in, then repeat until you've filled all the balls.

Now you're ready to coat the arancini. In a small bowl, mix the chickpea flour with enough water to give it a sticky egg-like consistency. Put the breadcrumbs into another bowl. Carefully dip each arancini into the wet flour mixture, then gently roll in the breadcrumbs, making sure each one is well coated, then transfer to a plate as you go. Repeat until you've coated all the balls.

Either heat the oven to 180°C (350°F) then bake the arancini on a lined baking tray for 15 minutes, or you can deep fry them in vegetable oil. I set my deep-fat fryer to 170°C (340°F) and fry them for 4 minutes, or until golden and crisp.

Quickly fry the sage leaves in the oil that you're frying your arancini in or, if baking, simply heat a non-stick frying pan over a medium heat, add a touch of oil, then fry the sage leaves for a few seconds until crisp. Transfer to a plate lined with kitchen paper to drain.

Serve the hot arancini straight away with the crispy sage and my cranberry sauce alongside!

Parsnip and Vanilla Soup

Believe it or not, parsnip and vanilla complement each other really well. This soup is so luxurious it'll charm your diners.

2 tbsp olive oil or water
4 banana shallots, finely chopped
1 garlic clove
8 parsnips, peeled and chopped into
    2cm (¾in) pieces
2 sprigs of fresh thyme
440ml (scant 2 cups) vegetable stock
440ml (scant 2 cups) almond milk
1 vanilla pod

3 tbsp lemon juice
sea salt and pepper

To serve
60g (½ cup) hazelnuts
50g (½ cup) dried cranberries
a few sprigs of fresh thyme or rosemary
good olive oil

Serves
6

Cooks In
40 minutes

Difficulty
2/10

GF

Heat the oil or water in a saucepan over a medium heat, then sweat the shallots and garlic until translucent. Add some seasoning, the parsnips and thyme sprigs.

Turn the heat down very low and cover the saucepan. Sweat the parsnips until they're almost soft, stirring often, for about 15 minutes.

Add the stock and milk, and stir to combine. Spilt the vanilla pod down the middle lengthways and scrape out the seeds using the back of your knife. Add the seeds and the pod to the saucepan, bring the soup to the boil, then take it off the heat and scoop out the vanilla pod.

Carefully pour the soup into a blender and blend until smooth. Pour the soup back into your saucepan and check the seasoning, adding salt, pepper and the lemon juice to bring out the flavours.

Serve in warmed bowls or mugs, sprinkled with the hazelnuts and cranberries, a sprig or two of herbs and a drizzle of good-quality olive oil.

Sweet Cranberry Glazed BBQ "Ribs"

I unleashed this recipe on my YouTube channel to rave reviews!
This slightly refined version makes a perfect starter or party food.

For the "ribs"
300ml (1¼ cups) hot vegetable stock
10g (½ cup) dried mushrooms
3 tbsp vegetable oil
1 onion, finely chopped
2 garlic cloves, finely chopped
100g (½ cup) chickpeas (garbanzos)
3 tbsp tomato purée
1 tbsp soy sauce
1 tbsp maple syrup
1 tbsp miso
2 tsp liquid smoke
¼ tsp sea salt
¼ tsp pepper
3 tsp smoked paprika
1 tsp fennel seeds
½ tsp allspice
1 tbsp chilli flakes
290g (2¼ cups) vital wheat gluten

For the cranberry BBQ sauce
225g (1 cup) tomato ketchup
2 tsp English mustard
1 tbsp balsamic vinegar
4 tbsp Cranberry and orange sauce
   (page 114)
2 drops liquid smoke (optional)
3 tbsp coconut sugar
1 tbsp cumin
1 tsp garlic powder
½ tsp allspice
sea salt and pepper
360ml (1½ cups) cola
1 bay leaf
1 star anise

Serves
8

Cooks In
3 hours

Difficulty
7/10

Preheat your oven to 160°C (325°F). Mix the hot vegetable stock with the dried mushrooms in a small bowl and set aside for 5 minutes for the mushrooms to rehydrate.

Heat 1 tablespoon of oil in a small saucepan, sauté the onion and garlic until softened and lightly golden, then spoon into a blender with the garlic, chickpeas, tomato purée, soy sauce, maple syrup, miso, liquid smoke, salt, pepper, paprika, fennel seeds, allspice and chilli flakes, plus the mushrooms and stock. Blitz until smooth.

Put the vital wheat gluten in a large mixing bowl. Pour in the wet mixture and stir with a spatula until everything is well combined and forms a dough.

Tip the dough onto a clean work surface and knead for around 12 minutes. Be firm – the tougher you are, the more meat-like texture your "ribs" will have when cooked. Once kneaded, leave the dough to rest for around 10 minutes.

Recipe continued overleaf

Sweet cranberry glazed BBQ "ribs" continued...

Mix together the BBQ sauce ingredients, except the cola, bay leaf and star anise, in a large bowl.

Shape the "rib" dough into a rectangle around 1cm (½in) thick and cut down the middle.

Preheat a griddle pan over a high heat and add the two tablespoons of oil. Brush some BBQ sauce over each piece of dough and lay these on the pan to grill for 2–3 minutes on each side. Try to get some nice char lines. You may need to grill one piece of dough at a time, but once both pieces are charred, transfer them to a deep baking dish.

Mix the cola into the remaining BBQ sauce, then pour it over the dough. Add the bay leaf and star anise. Bake in the oven for 2 hours, carefully turning over the pieces of dough half way through cooking. Add a little water to the tray to stop the sauce from thickening too much. Once the "ribs" are cooked, remove the tray from the oven and leave to cool. I prefer to chill mine in the fridge overnight, then heat up in the oven for 10 minutes before serving, as the "ribs" will be firmer and more meat-like but you can also enjoy them straight from the oven.

Slice the "ribs" before serving and spoon the sauce over the top.

Sausage Rolls

These whole-food sausage rolls are rich and hit all the savoury notes of traditional sausage rolls. Legumes are great for us, and this is a great way of making them special for the holidays.

1 tbsp olive oil
1 red onion, finely sliced
1 red (bell) pepper, deseeded and finely diced
3 portobello mushrooms, finely chopped
3 garlic cloves, minced
zest of 1 lemon
2 tbsp fresh lemon thyme leaves
2 sprigs of rosemary, finely chopped
2 tsp sea salt
2 tsp cracked black pepper
3 tbsp sweet smoked paprika
1 x 400g (14oz) can of red kidney beans, drained, rinsed and patted dry
1 x 400g (14oz) can of chickpeas (garbanzos), drained, rinsed and patted dry

5 tbsp plain (all-purpose) flour, plus extra for dusting
70g (½ cup) walnuts, finely chopped (or use breadcrumbs if you need to keep it nut free)
1 sheet of ready-made vegan puff pastry
poppy seeds, for sprinkling
dipping sauce of your choice, to serve

For the pastry glaze
60ml (¼ cup) non-dairy milk
4 tbsp maple syrup
4 tbsp olive oil

Makes
20

Cooks In
90 minutes

Difficulty
7/10

Heat the oil in a large saucepan and sweat the onion, pepper, mushrooms, garlic, lemon zest, herbs, salt, black pepper and paprika over a medium heat until softened.

Meanwhile, combine the beans, chickpeas, flour and walnuts in a mixing bowl. Once the onion mixture has cooked, add it to the bowl. Use a potato masher to gently combine the mixture until it begins to hold together. Be careful not to over-mash it; you should aim to retain a chunky texture. Allow the mixture to cool completely.

Preheat your oven to 180ºC (350ºF). Whisk the glaze ingredients together in a small mixing bowl.

Lightly flour your work surface. Unroll the puff pastry and cut it into two long rectangles lengthways.

Recipe continued overleaf

Sausage rolls continued...

Shape half the filling into a sausage shape and position it along the centre of one of the rectangles. Brush the edges of the pastry with a small amount of the glaze, then roll the pastry over the filling to seal it completely. Use a fork to firmly press the pastry's edges together, and with a sharp knife, divide the roll into 10 pieces. Place these portions on your prepared baking tray, and repeat with the second sheet of pastry and remaining filling to form a total of 20 rolls. Allow the rolls to chill in the fridge for 20 minutes, as this will prevent them from bursting while baking. Alternatively, you can freeze them at this stage.

When you're prepared to bake, brush the tops and sides of the rolls with the remaining glaze and sprinkle poppy seeds over them.

Bake the rolls for about 35 minutes until they're golden brown, then serve with a dipping sauce of your choice.

Welsh Rarebits

Rarebit, is one of the classic Welsh dishes I grew up eating – it's basically fancy cheese on toast. When I stopped eating dairy I craved this nostalgic dish, but it's easy to achieve the flavours I once loved.

55g (¼ cup) plant-based butter
1 leek, finely sliced
2 garlic cloves, minced
3 tbsp plain (all-purpose) flour
125ml (½ cup) beer
2 tsp miso paste
1 tsp mustard
2 tbsp coconut aminos or soy sauce
180ml (¾ cup) non-dairy milk
juice of ½ lemon
30g (½ cup) nutritional yeast
sea salt and white pepper

a drizzle of olive oil
1 small sourdough loaf, cut into thick
   slices on an angle and toasted

For the caramelized red onions
2 tbsp olive oil
3 red onions, peeled, halved and finely sliced
4 tbsp coconut sugar or brown sugar
3 tbsp balsamic vinegar
2 sprigs of fresh thyme, leaves chopped, plus
   extra to garnish
pinch of sea salt and pepper

Serves
4

Cooks In
35 minutes

Difficulty
5/10

**Can be GF, if GF
bread is used**

First, prepare the caramelized onions. Heat the oil in a heavy-based saucepan over a medium heat, then add the onions. Cook for 3–4 minutes, stirring often, until they start to soften and colour.

Add the sugar, vinegar, thyme and seasoning, stir well and turn the heat down very low. Cover the saucepan and allow the onions to caramelize for 15–20 minutes – stir/shake the pan every now and then.

Meanwhile, melt the butter in a medium saucepan over a medium heat. Add the leek and garlic and sauté for 3–4 minutes until softened. Stir in the flour and let it cook out for 2 minutes before deglazing the pan with the beer. Cook off the alcohol for a few minutes before stirring in the miso, mustard and coconut aminos.

Add the milk and whisk until there are no lumps, then stir in the lemon juice, nutritional yeast and seasoning. Turn the heat down to low and let the sauce bubble away for a few minutes to thicken up.

Meanwhile, preheat your grill (broiler) to 180ºC (350ºF).

Heat the drizzle of olive oil in an oven-proof frying pan and toast the bread. Spoon lashings of the cheese sauce over each piece of toast, then put the pan under the grill to caramelize the tops.

When golden, serve up the rarebit with lots of the caramelized onions.

5-spice Pan-roasted Mushroom Wraps with Hoisin Sauce

When you cook mushrooms for long enough, they get crispy on the outside and a succulent centre. This recipe is inspired by Chinese crispy duck pancakes. Making your own 5-spice and hoisin sauce from scratch is simple and both can be stored for a while!

800g (28oz) mixed mushrooms,
4 tbsp sesame oil, for frying
6 Chinese pancakes (or large lettuce leaves, if gluten-free)
½ cucumber, cut into thin strips
1 carrot, peeled into ribbons
3 spring onions (scallions), cut into thin strips
155g (1 cup) raw cashew nuts, toasted
3 tbsp mixed sesame seeds, to sprinkle

For the hoisin sauce
1 tbsp tahini

4 tbsp soy sauce
2 tbsp dark brown sugar
½ tsp roasted garlic powder
1 tbsp sesame oil
2 tsp Sriracha
juice of ½ lime

For the 5-spice
2 star anise
2 tsp ground cinnamon
5 cloves
2 tsp fennel seeds
½ tsp ground ginger

Makes
6 wraps

Cooks In
45 minutes

Difficulty
5/10

Can be GF, if lettuce wraps are used

First up, mix together all the ingredients for the hoisin sauce in a small mixing bowl and set aside.

Put all the 5-spice ingredients in a pestle and mortar and grind them until you have a fine powder. Alternatively, put the ingredients in a spice blender and blitz until fine.

Trim off any roots from the mushrooms and brush off any dirt. Slice any king oysters lengthways, as they are a lot bigger than most other mushrooms.

Now for the fun part: grab a large, heavy-based, non-stick frying pan, place it over a high heat and add the oil. When the pan is smoking add all of the mushrooms – it may look like it is overfilled now but they will shrink an awful lot.

Grab another frying pan, or a saucepan, that's slightly smaller than the mushroom pan and sit it directly on top of the mushrooms. This is a technique I picked up from a big inspiration of mine, Derek Sarno. It will flatten the mushrooms and make sure they are all being seared completely. Leave the mushrooms for 4 minutes to cook, char and flavour up. Remove the top pan and flip over the mushrooms. Place the pan back on top and cook for a further 4 minutes. Don't worry if the mushrooms are a little blackened – it will add incredible flavour.

Recipe continued overleaf

5-spice pan-roasted mushroom wraps
with hoisin sauce continued...

Remove the top pan and stir in 1 tablespoon of the
5-spice mix and 2 tablespoons of the hoisin sauce. Place
the small pan back on top, turn the heat down low and
leave the mushrooms to cook for 12 minutes, stirring
every now and then.

The mushrooms should be glazed and charred with lovely
crispy bits. Spoon them out of the pan onto a chopping
board and roughly chop them up.

Gently heat your wraps in a pan or toaster (or wash your
lettuce leaves, if using). It's nice if you let your guests fill
their own wraps – add plenty of hoisin sauce, mushrooms,
cucumber, carrot, spring onions and toasted cashews then
sprinkle sesame seeds on top.

I like to use a mixture of bunashimeji, king oyster
(*eryngii*), oyster, enoki and maitake mushrooms –
packs of mixed mushrooms like these can be found
at most supermarkets.

Modern Quiche

Quiches have always been a family favourite, but I never thought we could have them again until I started experimenting. After a few attempts, I found that a combination of tofu, soy cream and gram flour really works to create an egg-like consistency once baked. Feel free to use shop-bought vegan shortcrust pastry to save time.

For the pastry
3 cups/375g plain flour
pinch of sea salt
1 cup/125g vegan margarine
3 tbsp nutritional yeast (optional)
2 tbsp non-dairy milk

(You can use shop-bought shortcrust vegan pastry, if you prefer.)

For the quiche "batter" mix
1 firm block tofu, all water removed
3 tbsp gram flour
¾ cup/180ml soy/oat cream
    (use milk if you don't have cream)
3 tbsp nutritional yeast
¼ tsp garlic powder
1 tsp miso paste
¼ tsp turmeric
1 tsp sea salt
½ tsp ground pepper

For the toppings
Be creative with your fillings and toppings, use ingredients you have to hand, or are in season. Ingredients that work well (enough to generously cover the top of your quiche) are:

baby potatoes, steamed and halved
red onion, chopped small
celeriac, pre-roasted
asparagus spears, halved lengthways
spring onions, halved lengthways
green beans, cut small
cherry tomatoes, halved
sun-dried tomatoes
olives
mixed fresh herbs

To garnish
pickles of your choice

Makes
6 mini 10cm (4in)
quiches or one
25cm (10in) quiche

Cooks In
90 minutes

Difficulty
7/10

First up, the pastry: place all the ingredients apart from the milk in a large mixing bowl. Rub the butter into the flour mix with your hands until the mix resembles a breadcrumb-like consistency.

Pour in a little milk to bring the mix together, to form a ball of dough. Give it a slight knead for 3–4 minutes on your work surface, then wrap in cling film (plastic wrap). Place the dough in the fridge to chill before rolling out.

Meanwhile, prepare the filling and preheat your oven to 180ºC (350ºF). In a blender, add the quiche "batter" mix ingredients and blitz until smooth and creamy. Set the mix aside.

Grease your tart cases or a loose bottom tart tin – I use a 23cm (9in) loose bottom cake tin.

Recipe continued overleaf

PARTY FOOD & LIGHT MEALS

Modern Quiche continued...

Roll out your pastry dough on lightly-floured greaseproof paper to around 3mm (⅛in) thick and large enough to fill the tin (or cases) and tin walls.

Carefully lift up the greaseproof paper and pastry, then turn it out over the tart tin (or cases), making sure the pastry is covering the whole tin, with a little excess. Gently peel away the greaseproof paper, and with a lightly-floured hand press the pastry into the corners of the tin. Cut away any overhanging bits of pastry.

Next you'll need to blind bake the pastry: place a large piece of greaseproof paper into the centre of the pastry, then fill it with a handful of dried beans or rice. Place the tart tin (or cases) onto a tray and into the oven to blind bake for 10 minutes.

After 10 minutes of cooking, remove the greaseproof paper and baking beans, then place the tray back into the oven to cook the pastry for a further 5 minutes, or until lightly golden.

Meanwhile stir the cooked potatoes, herbs and your other chosen toppings through the quiche "batter" mixture.

Once the pastry case/cases are cooked, remove them from the oven. Pour the quiche filling into the tart case/cases and smooth it out level. Neatly arrange your vegetable toppings within the quiche mix, pushing some down into the quiche "batter" and other toppings. Make sure you have a nice variety of colour, texture and flavours – be sure to include fresh herbs.

Turn the oven down to 160°C (325°F). Place the quiche(s) into the oven on the bottom shelf to cook for 40–45 minutes.

Once cooked, allow the quiche(s) to cool for at least an hour on a wire rack before serving warm, with pickles and additional herbs to garnish.

Smoked Chilli and Rosemary Dough-ball Fondue

This is a showstopper – light fluffy dough balls flavoured with beautiful smoky chilli and rosemary. Simple to make, and – paired with my "cheese" sauce – they are divine.

For the dough balls
500ml (2 cups) lukewarm water
2 tsp yeast
5 tbsp olive oil, plus extra for greasing
480g (3¾ cups) strong white bread flour, plus extra for dusting
2 tsp sea salt
1 tbsp dried rosemary
1 tbsp smoked chilli flakes

For the glaze
2 tbsp olive oil
4 tbsp non-dairy milk
4 tsp maple syrup or agave nectar

Toppings
1 tbsp sea salt
1 tbsp dried garlic flakes
1 tbsp smoked chilli flakes
a few sprigs of fresh lemon thyme and rosemary, leaves picked

For the "cheese" fondue
120g (½ cup) raw cashew nuts
250ml (1 cup) filtered cold water
1 tbsp tapioca starch
3 tbsp nutritional yeast
1 tsp English mustard
1 tsp white miso
pinch of sea salt and white pepper
¼ tsp onion powder

Serves
10

Cooks In
95 minutes
+ rising time

Difficulty
5/10

First make the dough balls: mix the lukewarm water with the yeast and olive oil, and leave it for around 10 minutes until slightly bubbly.

Combine the flour, salt, rosemary and chilli flakes in a large mixing bowl. Make a well in the middle, add the water and yeast mixture and stir until the mixture starts to form a dough.

Use your hands to form the dough, then tip it out onto a lightly floured work surface. Now it's time to knead. Knead the dough for around 8 minutes, when the dough should be smooth and quite elastic. Add minimal flour while kneading, if required. Lightly oil the bowl and put the dough back in, then place a clean damp tea (dish) towel over the top of the bowl and leave somewhere warm for around 1 hour, or until the dough has doubled in size.

After an hour, remove the dough from the bowl, knock the dough back and knead for 3 minutes.

Recipe continues overleaf

PARTY FOOD & LIGHT MEALS

Smoked chilli and rosemary dough-ball fondue continued...

Line a baking tray with greaseproof paper and place a lightly greased ramekin in the middle. This will eventually be the place for your "cheese" sauce/fondue to sit.

Cut the dough into approximately 25 even pieces – each piece should be about 35g (1¼oz). Use kitchen scales to weigh them. Roll each piece into a ball: the best way to do this is by putting one hand on top of the dough ball on the work surface, press down slightly and move your hand in a circular motion.

Neatly place the balls around the ramekin as you go. Once you've rolled all the balls, place the damp tea towel over the top and leave them somewhere warm to double in size. This should take around 30 minutes.

Preheat your oven to 200°C (400°F). Mix together the ingredients for the glaze in a small bowl and prepare the toppings.

When the dough balls have risen, use a pastry brush to brush some glaze over each one and sprinkle over the toppings. Bake in the preheated oven for 30 minutes on the bottom shelf.

While the dough balls are baking, make the "cheese" sauce/fondue. Soak the cashew nuts for around 10 minutes in boiling water, then drain away the water and add the softened nuts to a high-speed blender with all the other ingredients. Blend on full speed until you have a smooth mixture.

Pour the mixture into a non-stick saucepan and stir with a spatula over a medium heat. Be patient – you will be stirring for around 8 minutes. Stir until it has thickened but is still pourable.

Remove the dough balls from the oven and let them cool slightly. When they're cool enough to handle, pour the "cheese" sauce into the ramekin in the middle of the tray, sprinkle over a few extra chilli flakes, if you like, and serve.

Centre
Pieces

Shredded Mushroom "Meat"

A simple replacement to the usual meat on the dinner table;
this "turkey" seasoning makes the mushrooms tastier than ever.

500ml (2 cups) vegetable stock
25g (1 cup) dried mushrooms
1 tbsp miso paste
1 bay leaf
handful of fresh herbs, such as sage,
    thyme, rosemary, parsley
1 onion, halved
2 celery sticks, roughly chopped
10–15 king oyster mushrooms, or
    mushrooms of your choice (king oysters
    are best for this recipe but oyster, lion's
    mane and shiitake could also work)
3 tbsp olive oil

For the "turkey" seasoning
1 tsp dried thyme
2 tsp dried sage
1 tsp dried marjoram
1 tsp dried rosemary
2 tsp garlic granules or powder
1 tsp onion granules or powder
½ tsp smoked paprika
½ tsp ground white pepper
1 tsp sea salt

Serves
4–5

Cooks In
50 minutes

Difficulty
5/10

GF

Bring the vegetable stock to a simmer in a big pot and add the dried mushrooms, miso paste, bay leaf, herbs, onion and celery.

Simmer the broth for 5 minutes, before adding the fresh mushrooms. Poach the mushrooms for 5 minutes, then strain them from the broth. If all your mushrooms don't fit in at the same time, just poach them in batches. Reserve the leftover broth – this can be turned into a gravy.

Allow the mushrooms to cool until they're OK to handle, then, using a fork, shred and tear them into chunks.

Preheat your oven to 200ºC (400ºF).

Place a cast iron, or heavy-based, oven-proof frying pan over a high heat and add the oil. Add the shredded mushrooms and cook until golden and caramelized. Stir every now and then and press them using the back of your spatula to create more surface area to get caramelized and golden.

Meanwhile, toss together the seasoning in a small mixing bowl.

When the mushrooms are golden, stir through the seasoning, then place the pan into the oven and roast for 15 minutes.

Serve the mushrooms with your roast dinner or in a sandwich.

Whole Cauliflower Wellington Roast with Its Own Gravy

This is a bit of a tongue-in-cheek recipe – it almost shouldn't be allowed. It looks ridiculous really, but I love making underrated veg the centre of the dinner table.

2 carrots, roughly chopped
2 celery sticks, roughly chopped
1 leek, roughly chopped
250g (9oz) chestnut (cremini) mushrooms, roughly chopped
2 red onions, roughly chopped
3 garlic cloves
4 fresh thyme sprigs
2 tsp sea salt
1 medium cauliflower
juice of 1 lemon
1 x 500g (1lb 2oz) block of ready-made puff pastry
plain (all-purpose) flour, for dusting
Christmas trimmings of choice, to serve

For the cauliflower marinade
3 tbsp tomato purée (paste)
1 tbsp balsamic vinegar
2 tbsp maple syrup
1 tbsp dried sage
1 tbsp dried rosemary
1 tbsp olive oil
2 tbsp miso paste

For the duxelles
2 tbsp olive oil
200g (7oz) mushrooms, roughly chopped
2 shallots, roughly chopped
1 tbsp dried thyme
1 tbsp dried sage

For the spinach layer
1 tbsp olive oil
300g (10½oz) spinach
pinch of sea salt

For the gravy
3 tbsp tomato purée (paste)
3 tbsp plain (all-purpose) flour
360ml (1½ cups) white wine
2 tbsp Marmite or soy sauce
1 litre (4 cups) vegetable stock
pinch of sea salt and pepper

For the glaze
2 tbsp maple syrup
2 tbsp olive oil
2 tbsp soy milk

Serves
4–6

Cooks In
2 hours 30 minutes

Difficulty
7/10

Can be
GF

First up, preheat your oven to 180ºC (350ºF).

Mix together all the ingredients for the cauliflower marinade in a small mixing bowl.

Add the carrots, celery, leek, mushrooms, onions and garlic cloves to a large baking tray, and scatter over the thyme sprigs and salt. Place the cauliflower in the centre, so that it's surrounded by the roasting vegetables. Brush the marinade mixture over the cauliflower generously. Squeeze over the lemon juice, then place the tray into the oven to roast for 1 hour.

Recipe continues overleaf

***Whole cauliflower wellington roast
with its own gravy continued...***

Meanwhile, make the mushroom duxelles. Place a large non-stick frying pan over a medium heat and add the oil. When the pan is hot, add the mushrooms, shallots, thyme and sage and season with a little salt and pepper. Sauté the mixture for 4–5 minutes. When the mushrooms have caramelized, transfer the mixture to your food processor and blitz until it's lightly chopped. Set the mushroom mix aside too cool.

For the spinach layer, add the oil to the same frying pan placed over a high heat, then add the spinach. Sauté the spinach until it's wilted, adding a tiny pinch of salt while it is cooking. Once wilted, remove the spinach from the pan and place it onto a clean tea (dish) towel. Using the towel, squeeze the water out of the spinach, then set it aside to cool.

Once the cauliflower has been in the oven for an hour, remove it from the oven. Take the cauliflower out of the tray and set it aside to cool, leaving the remaining vegetables in the tray – these will form the base of the gravy.

To make the gravy, place the roasting tray over a low heat on your stovetop and add the tomato purée and flour. Cook for a minute or so, stirring, then deglaze the pan with the white wine, Marmite and vegetable stock. Scrape the bottom of the pan to release any flavourful roasting juices that may have stuck. Let the gravy bubble away and thicken up for 15 minutes or so. Once the gravy has thickened, pass it through a sieve into a saucepan. Check the seasoning, then set it aside until you're ready to serve.

Once the cauliflower, mushroom mixture and spinach have cooled, preheat your oven to 180ºC (350ºF). Whisk together the glaze ingredients in a small bowl.

Roll out your puff pastry on a lightly floured surface to around 3mm (⅛in) thick and big enough to be able to wrap up your cauliflower. Use a plate measuring about 25cm (10in) as a template to cut a circle shape in the centre of the pastry. Spread the mushroom duxelles mix into the middle of the pastry, leaving a 5cm (2in) border around the edge, then top with the spinach. Place the cauliflower on top, upside-down, then grab the edges of the pastry circle and wrap the cauliflower up.

Be creative with any excess pastry – you can cut shapes and top your wellington with them. Brush the whole wellington with your glaze.

Place the wellington onto a lined baking tray (the right way up) and then into the oven to roast for 30–35 minutes, or until the pastry is golden and crisp.

Serve the wellington right away with the gravy and all your Christmas trimmings.

The Ultimate Christmas Roast

This is Christmas, all wrapped up ... literally. My go-to centre piece recipe has all the flavours you think of when the holiday season is on your mind. The filling is succulent thanks to the vital wheat gluten.

For the "beef"
2 tbsp vegetable oil
1 onion, finely chopped
1 leek, finely chopped
2 garlic cloves, crushed
1 tsp sea salt
1 tsp cracked black pepper
pinch of cinnamon
pinch of allspice
pinch of paprika
pinch of ground nutmeg
1 tbsp dried sage
2 tsp dried rosemary
30g (¼ cup) dried cranberries
50g (½ cup) dried apricots
100g (1 cup) peeled and cooked chestnuts
240ml (1 cup) cider, from a 500ml
    (2-cup) bottle
240ml (1 cup) vegetable stock
1 tbsp miso paste
250g (2¼ cups) vital wheat gluten,
    plus extra if needed

For the spice rub
1 tsp cayenne pepper
1 tsp allspice
1 tsp dried sage
1 tsp dried rosemary
1 tsp dried tarragon

For roasting
remaining 260ml (1 cup) cider
1 orange, quartered
500ml (2 cups) vegetable stock
1 onion
2 garlic cloves
1 bay leaf
handful of fresh thyme and rosemary sprigs
1 tbsp miso paste
2 tbsp balsamic vinegar
320g (11¼oz) block ready-made
    vegan puff pastry
4 tbsp Cranberry and orange sauce
    (page 114)

For the glaze
3 tbsp maple syrup
3 tbsp non-dairy milk
4 tbsp vegetable oil

For the gravy
2 tbsp cornflour (cornstarch)
4 tbsp water

Method overleaf

Serves
6

Cooks In
2 hours 30 minutes

Difficulty
7/10

The ultimate Christmas roast continued...

Make the "meat" dough. Heat the oil a non-stick frying pan over a medium heat. Fry the onion, leek, garlic, seasoning, spices and herbs for 2–3 minutes.

Meanwhile put the cranberries, apricots and chestnuts into a blender and blitz until they're all a similar size. Add these to the frying pan and sauté for 3–4 minutes until everything has softened. Pour in the cider, stock and miso paste. Stir together and allow the mixture to simmer for 2 minutes before turning the heat off.

Once the wet mixture has cooled slightly, mix in the vital wheat gluten. It should form a nice dough. If your mix is too wet, add a little more vital wheat gluten. Tip the dough out onto a clean work surface and knead for 10 minutes. Leave to rest.

Preheat your oven to 170°C (340°F). Combine the rub spices in a bowl. Shape the dough into a sausage 10cm (4in) in diameter. Sprinkle the rub onto your work surface. Roll the dough in the rub.

Roll the dough in a piece of muslin (cheesecloth), twist the ends tightly, then tie each end with cook's string to secure it. Place the wrapped dough into a deep baking tray together with the rest of the roasting ingredients (except the pastry and cranberry sauce) and bake for 2 hours on the bottom shelf, turning over half way through to ensure it cooks evenly. Once baked, lift the roast out of the tray, reserving the roasting liquid, leave to cool slightly, then remove the muslin. At this point you can either chill it in the fridge for up to 3 days or continue. If you are not cooking now, make the gravy (below) and keep in the fridge, then reheat.

An hour before you want to serve, roll out your pastry into a rectangle about the size of a tea (dish) towel and around 3mm (⅛in) thick. Cut strips a third of the width of the pastry on each side, so you can cross them to make a lattice. Spread the cranberry and orange sauce over the roast, lift it into the centre of the pastry, wrap it up, then transfer to a baking sheet lined with non-stick baking paper. Combine the glaze ingredients in a bowl, then brush over the top of the pastry. Bake for 15–20 minutes, or until golden.

While the wellington is cooking, strain the roasting liquid from the baking tray through a sieve into a saucepan, pressing to squeeze out all the lovely juices. Place over a low heat and simmer for 10 minutes until you have a thick gravy. Mix the cornflour with the water and add it to the gravy while whisking until it thickens to your desired consistency. Remove the wellington from the oven, carve and serve with the rich gravy.

Slow-roasted Mushroom Fillet

When I travelled around Mexico, I saw so many *al pastor* restaurants, and I was determined to recreate the famous dish – with a holiday twist – using pressed mushrooms.

80ml (⅓ cup) olive oil
12 oyster mushroom clusters
2 sprigs of rosemary

For the herb mix
1 tbsp sweet smoked paprika
1 tbsp garlic granules
1 tbsp onion granules
1 tbsp dried sage
1 tbsp dried tarragon
1 tbsp dried thyme

1 tbsp dried marjoram
1 tbsp salt
2 tsp dried rosemary
1 tbsp cracked black pepper
½ tsp ground white pepper

For the glaze
3 tbsp maple syrup
1 tbsp olive oil
2 tsp miso paste
1 tbsp tomato purée (paste)

Serves
8–10

Cooks In
2 hours

Difficulty
7/10

GF

First up, mix together the herbs and spices for the herb mix in a small bowl.

Place a cast iron pan over a high heat and add a little of the oil. When the pan is hot, add a few mushroom clusters, being careful not to overcrowd the pan. Place another pan that is small enough to just fit inside the first pan on top – this compression will press the mushrooms flat, making sure they get extra meaty. If your top pan isn't that heavy, carefully apply some pressure with your hand (using a tea/dish towel so you don't burn your hand).

After 4–5 minutes of cooking and pressing, season the mushrooms in the pan generously with the herb mix, then flip them over. Continue to press the mushrooms for a further 5 minutes, making sure all the water has evaporated and they are going golden. Once the first batch has cooked, remove from the pan and set aside while you repeat the process with the rest of the mushroom clusters. Meanwhile, preheat your oven to 180ºC (350ºF).

When you've cooked and pressed all the mushrooms, it's time to carefully spear them onto a couple of skewers – use two skewers to create one large kebab. Press them together, compacting them as best as you can, then place the mushroom kebab onto a roasting tray.

Whisk the glaze ingredients together in a small mixing bowl, then brush the glaze onto the mushroom kebab using the rosemary sprigs. Place the kebab into the oven to roast for 35 minutes, brushing on a little more glaze half way through cooking.

Serve the mushroom fillet in front of your guests, carving it with a sharp knife. It can also be cooked on the barbecue – the smoke really infuses into the mushroom. Carving this giant kebab (or whatever you want to call it) at your dinner table will surely entertain.

CENTRE PIECES

Stuffed Roasted "Joint"

This is technical to make but so rewarding when you slice into it.
I believe this recipe is powerful enough to help reduce the amount
of people having meat on their dinner tables at Christmas –
the flavours are incredible!

For the "turkey"
240ml (1 cup) soy or oat milk
10g (½ cup) dried mushrooms
olive oil, for frying
1 onion, finely chopped, sautéed until soft
3 garlic cloves, finely chopped, sautéed
    until soft
120ml (½ cup) white wine
50g (¼ cup) canned chickpeas (garbanzos),
    drained and rinsed
110g (4oz) firm tofu, patted dry
3 tbsp white miso paste
2 tsp maple syrup
1 tbsp dried tarragon
1 tbsp dried thyme
2 tsp dried rosemary
1 tsp dried sage
1 tsp cayenne pepper
2 tsp sea salt
1 tbsp cracked black pepper
300g (2¾ cups) vital wheat gluten

For the broth
960ml (4 cups) vegetable stock
480ml (2 cups) white wine
2 sprigs of fresh rosemary
2 sprigs of fresh thyme
1 onion, quartered

handful of dried mushrooms
1 bay leaf
3 garlic cloves, peeled
pinch of sea salt and pepper

For the rub
4 tbsp mixed dried herbs
1 tsp cayenne pepper
½ tsp onion salt

For the stuffing
1 quantity Sweet potato and chestnut stuffing
    (page 118), skipping the final step

For the glaze
3 tbsp cranberry sauce
3 tbsp olive oil
1 tbsp tomato purée (paste)
1 tbsp soy sauce
2 tbsp maple syrup
pinch of sea salt and pepper

For the gravy
2 tbsp cornflour (cornstarch)
2 tbsp cranberry sauce
2 tbsp Marmite

Serves
8

Cooks In
2 hours

Difficulty
7/10

If you have a soy allergy, use 50g
(1¾oz) extra chickpeas instead of the
tofu. Use soy-free miso, or leave it out.

Stuffed roasted "joint" continued...

First up, you will need to make the "turkey": combine all the ingredients except the vital wheat gluten in a blender and blend until smooth. Transfer it to a large mixing bowl or a stand mixer (with the dough hook attached) and add the vital wheat gluten. Mixing slowly, combine everything to form a rough dough.

Tip the dough onto a clean work surface and knead for at least 10 minutes by hand, or do this in your mixer on medium speed. This is the most important part of the recipe – if you don't knead it properly you will be left with a horrible spongy texture. Be very firm!

Once kneaded, the dough should be quite firm and elastic. Use a rolling pin to bash and roll the dough into a rough rectangle around 1.25cm (½in) thick. Set the dough aside to rest for 10 minutes.

Add the broth ingredients to a large roasting tray, around 40 x 28 x 8cm (16 x 11 x 3in). Cut a piece of muslin (cheesecloth) slightly larger than the dough rectangle.

Mix the rub ingredients together in a small bowl, then sprinkle it over the dough. Cover the dough well in the spice mix, as this stops it sticking. Place the dough spice-side down onto the muslin.

Preheat your oven to 180°C (350°F). Spoon the stuffing across the middle of the dough and roll it up around the stuffing, moulding the edges together and sealing really well. Wrap the dough in the muslin as tightly as possible. Twist the ends, then tie them tightly with cook's string. Make sure your dough is a nice cylindrical shape.

Place the "joint" wrap into the roasting tray with the broth ingredients, then cover the tray with foil. Place the tray into the oven for 2 hours. Turn over half way through cooking and add additional stock if needed. Once cooked, use a slotted spoon to lift the "joint" out of the broth and, when cool enough to handle, carefully remove the muslin. The "joint" can now be wrapped in cling film (plastic wrap) and placed into the fridge until you're ready to serve it. Reserve the broth liquid as it makes a great gravy.

An hour before you want to serve, preheat your oven to 180°C (350°F).

Place the "joint" in a large baking tray. Mix all the ingredients for the glaze together, then brush lashings of it all over the "joint". Bake for 25 minutes.

While the "joint" is cooking, add the reserved broth liquid to a saucepan and place it over a high heat to reduce it down until thick. If it's not thickening well, combine the cornflour with a splash of water, then add this to the gravy to help it thicken. Stir in the cranberry sauce and the Marmite for a richer flavour.

Serve the roasted joint straight away, sliced and with all the trimmings!

Rich White Wine Gravy

Packed full of umami flavour, this gravy goes well with all of the centre pieces in the book.

---

2 carrots, peeled
2 red onions, peeled
250g (9oz) chestnut (cremini) mushrooms
2 garlic cloves
1 leek
2 celery sticks
1 tbsp olive oil
pinch of sea salt and pepper
2 tbsp plain (all-purpose) flour
    (or gluten-free flour)
240ml (1 cup) vegan-friendly white wine

1 tbsp soy sauce
1 tbsp white miso paste
juice of 1 lemon
1 tbsp dried tarragon
2 sprigs of fresh thyme
2 sprigs of fresh sage
1 sprig of fresh rosemary
480ml (2 cups) vegetable stock

Serves
6

Cooks In
35 minutes

Difficulty
2/10

**Can be GF, if GF
flour is used**

Roughly chop the carrots, onions, mushrooms, garlic, leek and celery.

Heat the olive oil in a large saucepan over a medium heat. When the pan is hot, add the onions and mushrooms and sauté for 2 minutes until they've shrunk in size. Add the rest of the chopped vegetables and a pinch of seasoning and continue to sauté for 3 minutes, stirring often, until they caramelize, but make sure they don't burn. Stir in the flour and cook for 1 more minute.

Pour in the white wine and stir to deglaze the pan, then lower the heat. Add the soy sauce, miso paste and lemon juice, followed by the herbs. Cook for 2 minutes to allow the flavours to intensify, then add the vegetable stock. It's now time to leave the gravy to simmer and reduce down for 20 minutes.

The gravy should now be a lot thicker. Pour it through a fine sieve into a smaller saucepan, pressing with the back of a ladle to get as much of the liquid goodness out of the vegetables as possible. If the gravy is thinner than you'd like, simmer for a few more minutes for it to reduce some more.

Serve the gravy straight away or store in a sealed container in the fridge for up to 3 days, then reheat in a saucepan.

CENTRE PIECES

Stuffed
Squash Roast

What a beautiful array of flavours and colours,
all stuffed inside my favourite vegetable.

1 large butternut squash, washed
a little olive oil

For the glazed onions
2 red onions, finely sliced
3 tbsp balsamic vinegar
5 tbsp organic coconut sugar

For the Christmas rice
150g (¾ cup) wild rice, cooked
150g (5½oz) whole cooked vacuum-packed
    chestnuts, roughly chopped
75g (2½oz) dried apricots, chopped
150g (1 cup) mixed nuts, chopped
pinch of cayenne pepper

pinch of paprika
juice of ½ lemon
pinch of sea salt and pepper
pinch of dried sage

For the sautéed mushrooms
160g (1½ cups) fresh mushrooms
    (I used girolles)
1 tsp roasted garlic powder
sea salt and pepper
5 tbsp Cranberry and orange sauce (page 114)
4 peppers, roasted, skin removed
6 sun-dried tomatoes, re-hydrated
2 handfuls of baby spinach

Serves
6

Cooks In
70 minutes

Difficulty
5/10

GF

Preheat your oven to 180°C (350°F). Split the squash in half lengthways, place cut-side up onto a baking tray and bake for 45 minutes, or until just soft.

Meanwhile, make the glazed onions. Heat 3 tablespoons of water in a non-stick saucepan, add the sliced onions and sweat for 5 minutes. Add the vinegar and sugar, then cook for a further 10 minutes over a low heat, stirring occasionally, until caramelized. Set aside.

Mix the Christmas rice ingredients in a mixing bowl until fully combined, then set aside.

Sauté your mushrooms. Heat 2 tablespoons of water in a non-stick frying pan over a medium heat. Add the mushrooms, garlic powder and seasoning. Sauté for 5 minutes.

When the squash is cooked and cooled slightly, scoop out the seeds, then scoop out a 2cm (1in) channel of flesh and mix that into the Christmas rice mixture. Spoon the cranberry sauce into one of the squash halves, followed by the rice. Top with the roasted peppers, onions, mushrooms, sun-dried tomatoes and spinach. Place the other squash half on top, tie together in three places and roast for a further 15 minutes. Carve and serve straight away.

Rosemary, Red Wine and Garlic "Beef" with Rich Jus

Packed with hearty flavours, this "beef" roast is seriously good.
The broth reduces down to create the ultimate jus. You can make
the "beef" up to three days in advance of serving, providing you
store it in the fridge.

For the "beef"
160ml (⅔ cup) hot vegetable stock
10g (½ cup) dried porcini
olive oil, for frying
1 red onion, finely chopped
3 garlic cloves, finely chopped
120ml (½ cup) red wine
50g (¼ cup) chopped cooked beetroot (beet)
50g (½ cup) canned black beans,
    drained and rinsed
2 tbsp tomato purée (paste)
1 tbsp Dijon mustard
2 tbsp balsamic vinegar
1 tbsp miso paste
2 tsp Marmite
3 tsp dried mixed herbs
1 tsp cayenne pepper
3 tsp dried rosemary
2 tsp sea salt
1 tbsp cracked black pepper
360g (3 cups) vital wheat gluten

For the broth
720ml (3 cups) vegetable stock
480ml (2 cups) red wine
1 tbsp miso paste
1 onion, peeled and quartered
3 garlic cloves, peeled

1 bay leaf
3 sprigs of fresh rosemary
4 tbsp dried mushrooms
2 tsp cornflour (cornstarch), optional
1 tbsp Cranberry and orange sauce
    (page 114)

For the herb coating
¼ tsp dried sage
¼ tsp dried oregano
¼ tsp cayenne pepper
¼ tsp dried rosemary
¼ tsp dried tarragon
1 tbsp cracked black pepper

For roasting
2 tbsp wholegrain mustard
2 tsp cracked black pepper
2 tbsp smoked olive oil (or olive oil)

To serve
sprig of fresh rosemary
sea salt flakes

Method overleaf

Serves
8–10

Cooks In
2 hours

Difficulty
7/10

***Rosemary, red wine and garlic "beef" with
rich jus continued...***

First make the "beef". Pour the hot vegetable stock over the porcini in a small bowl and set aside for 5 minutes for the porcini to rehydrate.

Heat a splash of olive oil in a non-stick saucepan. Add the onion and garlic, reduce the heat and allow them to soften for 2 minutes, stirring often. Remove from the heat and tip them into a blender with the porcini and soaking liquid, plus all the remaining "beef" ingredients, except the vital wheat gluten. Let the mixture cool for 5 minutes before you blitz.

Blitz the wet ingredients together until smooth, then pour into a large mixing bowl, add the vital wheat gluten and quickly stir with a spatula until everything is well combined into a dough.

Using an electric stand mixer with a dough hook, knead on medium speed for 10 minutes. If hand kneading, knead the dough on your work surface for 12 minutes. Return the dough to the bowl and cover with a clean tea (dish) towel to rest and firm up for 15 minutes.

Meanwhile, heat all the broth ingredients, except the cranberry sauce, in a saucepan, bring to the boil, then reduce to simmering.

Shape the dough into a rough fillet shape to make it easier for wrapping in pastry. Mix the herb coating ingredients together, then sprinkle it onto your work surface and roll the fillet in it.

Wrap the fillet in muslin (cheesecloth) and tie the ends with cook's string – this holds the shape. Lower the fillet into the simmering broth, pop the lid on and cook for 1 hour 15 minutes until firm to touch. Make sure the broth is simmering, never boiling. Carefully turn the fillet over a couple of times so that it cooks evenly. Once cooked, remove from the broth and, when cool enough, remove the muslin.

Strain the broth into a saucepan. Heat gently until it has reduced and thickened to form a jus. Add a little cornflour (cornstarch) blended with cold water if it's not thickening. Stir in the cranberry sauce for a touch of sweetness.

One hour before serving, preheat your oven to 180°C (350°F). Spread the mustard over the fillet and sprinkle over the black pepper. Heat a large ovenproof pan on a high heat, add the oil and brown the fillet on all sides. Transfer the pan to the oven and roast for 15–20 minutes. Top with a sprig of fresh rosemary and a sprinkle of sea salt. Slice into thick pieces and serve with the jus in a jug ready for pouring.

Stuffed Aubergine Platter

A lighter option for your Christmas spread, but no compromise
on taste. Make sure you char the aubergines before baking
– it adds loads of flavour.

1 tbsp miso paste
2 tbsp maple syrup
3 tbsp olive oil
4 aubergines (eggplants), cut in half
    lengthways

For the stuffing
1 tbsp olive oil
1 red onion, cubed
1 garlic clove, crushed
1 red (bell) pepper, cubed
1 courgette (zucchini), cubed
1 sprig of fresh rosemary, leaves picked,
    finely chopped
1 tbsp fresh thyme leaves
¼ tsp ground cinnamon
¼ tsp ground allspice
½ tsp cayenne pepper
zest of 1 orange
4 tomatoes, cubed
225g (1½ cups) quinoa or couscous, cooked

4 tbsp pine nuts
1 tsp sea salt
1 tsp black pepper

For the parsnip crisp (optional)
1 parsnip, peeled
3 tbsp vegetable oil
pinch of sea salt and pepper

For the tahini dressing
3 tbsp tahini
120ml (½ cup) cold water
juice of ½ lemon
½ tsp ground cumin
pinch of sea salt and pepper

To serve
fresh thyme leaves
seeds of ½ pomegranate
handful of walnuts, toasted

Serves
4

Cooks In
60 minutes

Difficulty
2/10

GF

Line a baking tray with non-stick baking paper and
preheat your oven to 180°C (350°F).

In a small mixing bowl, whisk together the miso, maple
syrup and 2 tablespoons of the oil with a fork or small
whisk until smooth.

Heat a griddle pan and add the remaining oil. When the
pan is very hot, add the aubergines, cut-side down (do
this in batches if your pan is small). Char the aubergines
for around 3 minutes on both sides, transferring to the
lined baking tray, cut-side up, as you go.

Generously spread the miso mix over the top of the
aubergines, then pop them into the oven to cook through
for 10 minutes.

Recipe continues overleaf

Stuffed aubergine platter continued...

Meanwhile make the stuffing. Heat the oil in a large non-stick frying pan over a medium heat. Add the onion, garlic, red pepper and courgette and fry, stirring, for 2 minutes before adding the herbs, spices and orange zest. Cook for 4–5 minutes more, until softened. Stir in the tomatoes, quinoa, pine nuts and seasoning, then turn off the heat.

Remove the aubergines from the oven. Carefully (as they are very hot) use a fork to squish down the flesh in the centre of the aubergines, leaving a 1cm (½in) border all around the edge. (I much prefer doing it this way as I don't want to lose any of the flavour, which could happen if you scoop the filling out the traditional way.)

Spoon the vegetable stuffing mix generously into the aubergines, then place them back into the oven for a further 15 minutes.

If you are serving your stuffed aubergines with crispy parsnips, make them now. Use a swivel peeler to peel the parsnip flesh into ribbons. Add them to a bowl and pour over the oil. Sprinkle with the seasoning and give it a good mix, making sure all the ribbons are well coated.

Line a baking tray with greaseproof paper and spread out the parsnip ribbons. You don't have to be overly neat, just make sure they aren't all on top of one another. Bake in the oven on the middle shelf for 10–12 minutes. Alternatively, for extra crispy parsnips, you can shallow fry them. Heat your oil to around 180°C (350°F), then carefully place the parsnip ribbons into the oil to fry for 3–4 minutes, or until golden. Remove the ribbons from the oil using a slotted spoon and place them onto a plate lined with kitchen paper. The parsnips will crisp up after a couple of minutes of cooling.

Just before serving, mix together all the ingredients for the tahini dressing with a fork in a small mixing bowl. Check the seasoning before serving.

When the aubergines are ready, arrange them on a serving platter, generously topped with the tahini dressing, crispy parsnips, fresh thyme, pomegranate seeds and toasted walnuts.

Festive Nut Roast Wreath

Well, it wouldn't be a plant-based Christmas without a nut roast!
Roasted in a wreath tin and topped with my cranberry sauce,
it's the perfect Christmas centre piece.

---

3 tbsp olive oil
1 red onion, finely chopped
1 celery stick, finely chopped
2 garlic cloves, chopped
1 leek, finely chopped
200g (7oz) butternut squash, peeled,
    and cut into small cubes
1 small aubergine (eggplant), cut into
    small cubes
60g (2oz) vacuum-packed chestnuts,
    roughly chopped
½ tsp allspice
¼ tsp ground cinnamon
1 sprig of fresh rosemary, finely chopped
10 fresh sage leaves, finely chopped
sea salt and pepper
1 orange, zest and juice
140g (1 cup) mixed nuts (Brazil nuts,
    pistachios, walnuts, etc.)
165g (1 cup) cooked chickpeas (garbanzos)

45g (½ cup) gluten-free breadcrumbs
50g (⅓ cup) dried cranberries,
    roughly chopped
50g (¼ cup) dried apricots, roughly chopped
50g (⅓ cup) sun-dried tomatoes,
    roughly chopped
3 tbsp balsamic vinegar
1 tbsp white miso paste
3 tbsp nutritional yeast
1 tbsp Marmite

For the cranberry topping
6 tbsp Cranberry and orange sauce
    (page 114)

Optional garnishes
fried sage leaves (page 119)
shelled pistachios
dried oranges
fresh rosemary

Serves
6

Cooks In
70 minutes

Difficulty
5/10

GF

Preheat your oven to 180°C (350°F). Grease a non-stick 25cm (10in) cake ring mould/tin. (Line with baking paper if it's not non-stick.)

Heat the olive oil in a large saucepan over a medium heat and sauté the onion, celery, garlic, leek, squash, aubergine and chestnuts for a few minutes, stirring frequently. Add the spices, herbs, some seasoning and the orange zest and juice. Turn the heat down and cook for 8–10 minutes, stirring every now and then. You want all the flavours to marry together and the vegetables to soften slightly.

While the vegetables are cooking, blitz the nuts in a blender until they are a crumb-like consistency. Add the chickpeas and pulse a couple times just to break them down slightly. Tip these into the saucepan and add the breadcrumbs, cranberries, apricots and sun-dried tomatoes, stirring well.

Recipe continues overleaf

Festive nut roast wreath continued...

Add the vinegar, miso paste, nutritional yeast and Marmite and cook for 3–4 minutes, stirring often, then turn off the heat.

Spoon the Cranberry and orange sauce into the tin and spread out evenly, then carefully spread the nut roast mixture on top. Press the mix into the tin as much as you can. Once you've filled the tin, cover it over with foil and roast in the preheated oven for 30–35 minutes.

After roasting, allow to cool slightly before turning out of the tin. Serve your festive nut roast wreath topped with your chosen garnishes.

Rich Portobello Mushroom and Lentil Spiral

Lentils are so underrated: when cooked down with mushrooms, red wine, garlic and herbs, they are so rich. Then wrapped in crisp pastry, this dish is a show stopper.

3 tbsp olive oil, plus extra for greasing
1 onion, finely diced
2 garlic cloves, minced
1 celery stick, finely diced
1 carrot, peeled and finely diced
5 Portobello mushrooms, cleaned, trimmed
    and cut into 1cm (½in) cubes
2 tsp cracked black pepper
5 tbsp plain (all-purpose) flour (or gluten-free
    flour), plus extra for dusting
240ml (1 cup) red wine
720ml (3 cups) vegetable stock
300g (1½ cups) cooked puy lentils, rinsed
2 tbsp soy sauce or coconut aminos
1 tbsp Marmite or miso paste
2 tbsp fresh thyme leaves
1 tbsp fresh rosemary, finely chopped

1 tbsp dried tarragon
1 bay leaf
2 tsp dried sage
1 tbsp redcurrant jelly, or my Cranberry
    and orange sauce (page 114)
10 sheets filo (phyllo) pastry
sea salt

For the glaze
60ml (¼ cup) non-dairy milk
4 tbsp maple syrup
4 tbsp olive oil

To serve
Celeriac purée (page 113)
Pan-roasted pumpkin wedges (page 119)

Serves
6

Cooks In
2 hours

Difficulty
7/10

First up make the rich filling (which I usually make the day before serving). Preheat a large saucepan over a medium heat and add the oil. When it's hot, add the onion, garlic, celery and carrot. Sauté for 3 minutes or until soft and golden. Add the mushrooms and let them cook for a good 5 minutes to remove the excess water from them and so that they colour nicely, which will give the filling a great depth of flavour.

Once the mushrooms have coloured, add a pinch of the cracked black pepper, then stir in the flour. Turn the heat down and stir the mix for 2–3 minutes for the flavour of the flour to cook out.

Deglaze the pan with the red wine and stock, stirring well and scraping any bits off the bottom of the pan using your spoon. Add the lentils, soy sauce, Marmite, herbs and redcurrant jelly and the rest of the black pepper. Pop the lid on and allow the mix to cook for 15–20 minutes, stirring every now and then. If it gets too thick, add a touch more stock.

Recipe continues overleaf

CENTRE PIECES

*Rich portobello mushroom and
lentil spiral continued...*

Once the lentils are tender, give it a taste and season with
salt if you need to. When you're happy, remove the mix
from the pan and allow to cool completely. Ideally let it
chill in the fridge overnight.

2 hours before serving, preheat your oven to 180ºC
(350ºF) and grease a 20cm (8in) round oven dish.

Mix together your glaze ingredients and grab a
pastry brush.

Unroll your filo pastry and place one sheet on a lightly
floured surface with a long side towards you. Brush it with
glaze, then place a line of the filling mix along the bottom
edge of the pastry – be generous, but not too generous
– then simply roll up. Spin the roll up into a spiral and
place it into the centre of your greased dish. Continue to
wrap and roll until you've used all the mix and filled up
your oven dish with one large spiral.

Brush more glaze over the top, then place the pie into
your oven for about 25 minutes until the pastry is light
golden and crisp. Serve with celeriac purée and roasted
pumpkin wedges.

Shallot
Tarte Tatin

Unveil this tarte tatin to your guests and you will be worshipped!

4 tbsp olive oil

5–6 banana shallots, peeled, cut in half
lengthways, roots trimmed

3 tbsp soft brown sugar

4 tbsp balsamic vinegar

2 tbsp vegan-friendly brandy
(optional)

2 sprigs of fresh thyme

1 sprig of fresh rosemary

½ tsp sea salt

½ tsp cracked black pepper

320g (11¼oz) ready-made vegan puff pastry
plain (all-purpose) flour, for rolling

Serves

4

Cooks In

60 minutes

Difficulty

7/10

**Can be GF, if GF
pastry is used**

Preheat your oven to 170°C (340°F). Roll out the pastry on a lightly floured surface to around 4mm (⅛in) thick, then cut it into a circle about 2.5cm (1in) wider than your pan.

Heat your ovenproof, heavy-based frying pan over a medium heat and heat 3 tablespoons of the oil. Add the shallots, cut-side up, making sure you have enough to fill the base. Cook for 3–4 minutes, then sprinkle over the brown sugar. Flip over the shallots using a palette knife – arrange them neatly, so that the base is covered and there aren't any gaps.

Turn the heat down low, then add the balsamic vinegar and brandy, if using. (Allow the alcohol to cook off, leaving behind the sweet brandy flavour.) Add the leaves from one sprig of thyme and the rosemary and let the onions caramelize for 4–5 minutes. Sprinkle over the salt and pepper, then turn off the heat and drizzle the remaining oil on the top.

Carefully lift your pastry and lay it over the pan. Quickly and carefully tuck the pastry down right into the edges, using a wooden spoon so you don't have to touch the hot pan, then pop into the oven to bake for 25–30 minutes, or until the pastry is lovely and golden.

Once cooked, remove the tart from the oven and allow it to cool for 2–3 minutes. Place a plate on top of the pan (make sure it's larger than the pan!), wear an oven glove to protect the arm holding the board (some caramel goodness may drip out and it's super-hot), then quickly, carefully and confidently flip the pan and plate to turn it out.

Serve straight away. This tart tastes amazing with Truffle cream "cheese" (page 169) and the remaining fresh thyme.

CENTRE PIECES

All the
Trimmings

Pommes Anna

Layer upon layer of delicious creamy potatoes, subtly spiced with elegant saffron. I could eat trays and trays of this.

330g (1½ cups) plant butter
5 garlic cloves, minced
1 large leek, very finely sliced
1 tsp saffron threads
1 tbsp sea salt
1 tsp ground white pepper
1kg (2lb 4oz) Maris Piper
   potatoes

Serves
6

Cooks In
2 hours

Difficulty
7/10

GF

Preheat your oven to 180ºC (350ºF) and line a medium–large ovenproof dish, at least 2cm (¾in) deep, with greaseproof paper.

Add the butter, garlic, leek, saffron, salt and pepper to a saucepan, then place over a low heat to infuse for 15 minutes.

Meanwhile peel and finely slice your potatoes using a mandoline.

Place the sliced potatoes into a large mixing bowl, pour over the infused butter and mix well. Transfer the potato and butter mixture to the lined baking tray or pan.

Cover the potatoes with a sheet of greaseproof paper, then place a similar-sized baking tray on top, followed by a few oven-proof weights (I use a couple of baking dishes). Place the tray into the oven for 55 minutes.

Once the potatoes are tender, remove the tray from the oven and turn the oven to the grill (broiler) function. Remove the weights, top tray and greaseproof paper and place the potatoes under the grill for around 5–6 minutes to caramelize on top.

When golden and crisp, serve up.

Chorizo-flavour Carrots

This is a fun way of taking my deliciously sweet homegrown carrots to the next level. Creating this smoky, rich cooking liquor gives the carrots a coating that has all the notes of chorizo.

8 carrots (ideally 13cm/5in long and
    1.5cm/½in thick), peeled and trimmed
splash of olive oil
5 tbsp pomegranate seeds
4 tbsp pistachio nuts, roughly chopped

For the broth
440ml (scant 2 cups) vegetable stock
250ml (1 cup) orange juice

1 tbsp miso paste
5 tbsp sweet smoked paprika
1 onion, quartered
5 garlic cloves, crushed
2 tbsp smoked sea salt (use normal sea
    salt if you don't have smoked)
2 tbsp fennel seeds
1 bay leaf
handful of fresh oregano

Serves
4

Cooks In
30 minutes

Difficulty
3/10

Add all the broth ingredients to a saucepan big enough to fit the carrots in and place it over a medium heat. When the broth starts to simmer, add the carrots. Let the carrots cook in the broth for 15 minutes.

When the carrots are tender, remove them from the broth. Allow the broth to continue to bubble away and reduce down and thicken up.

Place a large non-stick frying pan or griddle pan over a medium heat and add a splash of oil. When the pan is hot, add the carrots and sauté them for 3–4 minutes or until caramelized. Then add the reduced broth and let it bubble and coat the carrots really well.

Serve the carrots topped with the pomegranate seeds and pistachio nuts.

Braised Leeks with Crispy Leek

Double leek goodness! Slow cooking the leeks creates a melt-in-the-mouth luxurious texture, finished with a caramelized crispy leek.

5 medium leeks
4 tbsp olive oil
6 sage leaves
2 garlic cloves
375ml (1½ cups) white wine
250ml (1 cup) vegetable oil
3 tbsp cornflour (cornstarch)
2 tbsp chives, finely chopped
sea salt and pepper

Serves
4

Cooks In
45 minutes

Difficulty
3/10

GF

Top and tail the leeks and split them down the middle. Wash the leeks to remove any dirt or grit from their layers. Save any green parts for stock, soups and stews and set aside half a leek for the crispy leek topping.

Place a large – ideally cast iron – pan over a medium heat and add the olive oil, sage and garlic. Let the garlic and sage cook for a minute to infuse their flavour into the oil, then add the leek halves, cut side down. Cook the leeks for around 4 minutes, then carefully flip them over. Season them with salt and pepper, then deglaze the pan with the white wine. Turn the heat down to low, then pop a lid on the pan and let the leeks braise for 25 minutes.

Meanwhile, to make the crispy leek topping, add the vegetable oil to a saucepan and place over a low heat.

Cut the reserved leek half into extra fine slices on the angle to achieve long leek slithers. Add the cornflour to a small bowl and toss the leek in it, making sure each slice is coated.

When the oil is hot, fry the leek slices in the oil, using a slotted spoon to carefully stir to make sure they're all getting nice and golden. When crisp, remove the leeks from the oil and place them onto a plate lined with kitchen paper.

Serve the braised leeks in the pan, topped with fresh chopped chives and the crispy leeks.

Maple and Sriracha-glazed Crispy Brussels Sprouts

Honestly, I didn't like sprouts until I made them this way. Coating them in cornflour before frying creates the most mind blowing crispy texture, and just before serving, toss them in the glaze.

350g (12oz) Brussels sprouts,
  trimmed and halved
4 tbsp cornflour (cornstarch)
80ml (⅓ cup) vegetable oil
roasted peanuts, crushed,
  to garnish

For the glaze
5 tbsp maple syrup
3 tbsp sriracha sauce
1 tbsp soy sauce
½ tsp onion granules
½ tsp garlic granules

Serves
4

Cooks In
20 minutes

Difficulty
3/10

Can be
GF

Steam or boil the sprouts until just cooked – this should take 4–5 minutes. Once cooked, remove them from the pan and allow to steam dry.

Meanwhile, stir together the glaze ingredients in a large mixing bowl.

Toss the steam-dried sprouts in the cornflour so that they're lightly coated.

Place a wok or large frying pan over a medium heat and add the oil. When the oil is hot, add the sprouts and allow them to fry until they're crispy and golden. Add the sauce and toss for 2–3 minutes, until the sprouts are glazed.

Serve right away, topped with crushed peanuts.

Pumpkin Mac and Cheese with Pulled BBQ Shrooms

I wasn't going to include this recipe, but each year, close to Thanksgiving, my lovely Stateside audience demand a mac and cheese recipe from me. I like to incorporate roasted pumpkin or squash into mine, then top with sticky BBQ mushrooms. It's comfort food at its finest.

55g (¼ cup) plant butter or 4 tbsp olive oil
1 onion, halved
200g (1 cup) cubed roasted pumpkin
2 garlic cloves, crushed
1 tbsp dried sage
½ tsp sweet smoked paprika
30g (¼ cup) plain (all-purpose) flour
750ml (3 cups) non-dairy milk
1 tbsp miso paste
1½ tsp sea salt
1 tsp ground white pepper

juice of ½ lemon
20g (3 tbsp) nutritional yeast flakes
2 tbsp Dijon mustard
300g (10½oz) macaroni pasta
4 tbsp panko breadcrumbs

For the pulled shroom brisket topping
250ml (1 cup) Cranberry BBQ Sauce (page 38), or shop-bought barbecue sauce
1 quantity Shredded mushroom "meat" (page 58)

Serves
6

Cooks In
70 minutes

Difficulty
5/10

Can be GF

Preheat your oven to 180ºC (350ºF).

Place a large saucepan over a low heat and add the butter or olive oil, followed by the onion, pumpkin and garlic. Sauté the mix for 5–6 minutes, then stir in the sage and paprika. Cook for another minute, then turn the heat down low and stir in the flour. Cook out the flour for a couple of minutes, then add the non-dairy milk, a little at a time. Bring the creamy sauce to a simmer, then stir in the miso, salt, pepper, lemon, yeast and mustard. Pop a lid on the pan and let the sauce cook away gently for 6–7 minutes, stirring every now and then until thickened.

Meanwhile, cook the macaroni in a large pan of water according to the instructions on the packet.

When the cheese sauce is creamy and luxurious, stir through the cooked pasta. Tip the mixture into a baking dish and sprinkle the breadcrumbs over the top. Place the mac and cheese in the oven and bake for 10 minutes.

Meanwhile, warm the barbecue sauce in a saucepan and stir in the mushroom meat until everything is heated through and the mushrooms are well glazed.

Remove the mac from the oven and top with the mushrooms. Place the mac back into the oven for 5 more minutes, then serve up.

Herb-crusted Cauliflower and Leek "Cheese"

This is creamy and cheesy, thanks to the coconut milk, miso and nutritional yeast. Of course, being a Welshman, I like to add leek as well. The herby breadcrumbs on top add a lovely crunch.

---

1 cauliflower, cut into florets
1 leek, sliced into 2cm (¾in) rounds

For the "cheese" sauce
400ml (14fl oz) can of coconut milk
5 tbsp nutritional yeast
80g (½ cup) raw cashew nuts,
    soaked in water
1 shallot
1 tbsp white miso paste
6 tbsp non-dairy milk
juice of ½ lemon

pinch of sea salt and pepper
1 garlic clove
1 bay leaf
2 sprigs of fresh thyme

For the herb coating
100g (1 cup) breadcrumbs
handful of fresh parsley
2 sprigs of fresh rosemary
handful of fresh sage leaves
4 sprigs of fresh thyme
3 tbsp olive oil

Serves
4

Cooks In
40 minutes

Difficulty
2/10

**Can be GF, if GF
breadcrumbs
are used**

First up, preheat the oven to 170°C (340°F) and heat a large saucepan of water until boiling. Add the cauliflower florets and leek slices and blanch for 3 minutes.

Meanwhile, put all the sauce ingredients, except the bay leaf and thyme, into a blender and blitz until smooth.

Lift out the cauliflower and leek with a slotted spoon into a bowl and set aside. Discard the water, place the pan back on a low heat and pour in the blended sauce. Add the bay leaf and thyme.

Clean out the blender and quickly blitz together the herb coating ingredients until you have fine crumbs.

Add the cauliflower and leek to the hot sauce, stir to combine everything, then tip the mixture into a 15 x 23cm (6 x 9in) ovenproof baking dish. Sprinkle over the herby breadcrumbs, then bake on the bottom shelf of the oven for 20 minutes, or until the topping is golden brown. Keep an eye on it – you don't want it to burn. Serve straight away.

Port and Balsamic Braised Red Cabbage

2 tbsp olive oil or water
1 red onion, finely sliced
1 red cabbage, finely shredded
2 crisp sweet apples, grated
    (Braeburns are ideal)
120ml (½ cup) vegan-friendly
    port
60ml (¼ cup) balsamic vinegar
zest and juice of 1 orange
100g (½ cup) soft brown or
    coconut sugar
1 star anise
1 cinnamon stick
1 tsp sea salt
2 tsp cracked black pepper
2 tbsp fresh thyme leaves,
    plus extra to garnish

Serves
6

Cooks In
60 minutes

Difficulty
2/10

GF

Heat the oil or water in a large, heavy-based, non-stick saucepan over a medium heat. Add the onion and sweat for 2–3 minutes, until soft and lightly golden.

Add the red cabbage and grated apple, turn the heat up and sauté for 3–4 minutes, stirring constantly.

The red cabbage will reduce in volume as it cooks – when it's half the original volume, turn the heat down low and pour in the port to deglaze the pan. Cook for a couple of minutes before adding the rest of the ingredients. Stir well, pop the lid on and leave the cabbage to cook for 55–60 minutes. Stir every now and then so it doesn't catch.

After an hour, the red cabbage should be tender and the liquid thickened to a glaze-like consistency. Sprinkle over a little extra fresh thyme before serving.

Sticky Beetroot with Walnuts

4 medium-sized mixed
    beetroots (beets)
3 tbsp olive oil or water
juice of ½ orange
3 tbsp maple syrup
2 tbsp balsamic vinegar
2 tbsp soy sauce or tamari
1 tsp cracked black pepper
100g (1 cup) walnut halves

Serves
4

Cooks In
60 minutes

Difficulty
2/10

GF

Preheat the oven to 180°C (350°F) and prepare the beetroots – wash and cut each one into 6–8 wedges, about 2.5cm (1in) thick.

Place the beetroot wedges in a deep ovenproof dish and add all the other ingredients except the walnuts. Mix everything together with your hands.

Place the dish into the oven and roast for 30 minutes, then remove the dish, mix in the walnuts and return to the oven for a further 15 minutes, or until the beetroots are tender.

Maple Pan-roasted Parsnips

Pan-roasting the parsnips this way not only creates a beautiful flavour, but saves space in your oven on Christmas Day.

---

6 parsnips, peeled and cut into batons, fibrous centres removed
1 tsp sea salt
1 tsp ground white pepper
3 sprigs of fresh thyme, leaves picked, plus extra for serving
½ lemon
3 tbsp olive oil
4 tbsp maple syrup

Serves
6

Cooks In
25 minutes

Difficulty
2/10

GF

Place the parsnips into a saucepan and cover with water. Add a pinch of the seasoning, the thyme and the lemon half. Cover and place over a high heat.

Bring the parsnips to a boil and cook for 4–5 minutes, then drain into a colander. You can cook the parsnips until this point the day before serving and keep covered in the fridge overnight.

About 25 minutes before serving, heat the oil in a large, non-stick saucepan over a medium heat. When it's hot, add the parsnips and toss or stir them often, cooking for 5–6 minutes. You want to get them nice and golden on all sides, but be careful, as they do burn quickly.

Once the parsnips are golden, add the maple syrup and the rest of the seasoning. Toss well, making sure the parsnips are all coated, and cook for a further 3 minutes. The maple syrup will caramelize and crisp up the parsnips!

Serve straight away topped with thyme leaves.

Photograph on page 107.

Sexy Sprouts

Even if you're not usually a sprout lover, I promise you will love these. Topping them with my smoky coconut bits just takes them to the next level.

500g (1lb) Brussels sprouts, trimmed
2 tbsp olive oil
200g (2 cups) vacuum-packed chestnuts, halved
1 tsp fennel seeds
handful of dried cranberries
zest of 1 lemon
pinch of sea salt and pepper

For the smoky coconut bits
100g (1 cup) coconut flakes
2 tbsp maple syrup
1 tbsp sweet smoked paprika
2 tbsp soy sauce
1 tbsp coconut oil

Serves
4

Cooks In
25 minutes

Difficulty
2/10

GF

Preheat the oven to 180°C (350°F) and line a baking tray with non-stick baking paper.

First up, make the smoky coconut bits. Put all the ingredients in a mixing bowl and stir well to coat the coconut flakes. Spread them out evenly over the lined baking tray and bake for 10–15 minutes, or until golden and crisp. Stir the coconut on the tray a couple of times during cooking to avoid it burning (which it can easily do).

For the sprouts, bring a large saucepan of water to the boil. Gradually add the sprouts to the water, making sure the water keeps at a rolling boil, and cook until tender and a vibrant green colour, usually around 3–4 minutes. Once the sprouts are cooked, drain and place them onto a tray lined with kitchen paper to soak up excess water if cooking straight away. Alternatively, you can chill the sprouts in the fridge at this stage until you're ready to flavour them up just before serving.

Before serving, heat the olive oil in a large wok over a high heat. Add the sprouts and sauté them for 2 minutes, then add the rest of the ingredients and continue to cook over a high heat, stirring often, for 3 more minutes. A little colour on the sprouts adds great flavour.

Once your sprouts are nicely coloured, throw in a handful of smoky coconut bits, saving the rest to sprinkle on top once you've dished up.

ALL THE TRIMMINGS

Orange-glazed Carrots

Jazz up your carrots by using orange juice – it helps them keep their sweetness and colour as well as creating the most amazing glaze. I like to use baby carrots for this dish.

300g (10½oz) carrots
480ml (2 cups) fresh orange juice
240ml (1 cup) vegetable stock
3 tbsp maple syrup
4 tbsp olive oil
handful of fresh thyme
1 tsp sea salt
1 tsp cracked black pepper
handful of pistachio nuts,
    to serve

Serves
6

Cooks In
20 minutes

Difficulty
2/10

GF

Peel your carrots if necessary and cut any large ones in half – make sure they're all a similar size. I use baby carrots, so I scrub them clean with a scourer and split any large ones lengthways.

Put the carrots in a large, lidded saucepan with the rest of the ingredients, cover and place over a high heat. If squeezing your own juice, add one of the orange halves to the pan for extra flavour. Cook the carrots until tender – baby carrots take around 8–10 minutes but it will depend on the size.

The orange sauce may have already reduced to a glaze-like consistency but if it hasn't, lift the carrots out of the pan with a slotted spoon (keep on a plate) and continue to cook until the liquid has reduced to a glaze. Once it has thickened, turn off the heat and return the carrots to the pan. Toss them in the glaze a few times until they are coated, then serve with pistachio nuts sprinkled over.

Gaz's Best-ever Roasties

Crispy on the outside, fluffy on the inside...
I love making (and eating!) these. Shaking them
in the pan roughs up the edges – vital for crispiness.

1kg (2.2lb) floury potatoes,
    such as Maris Piper, peeled
4 tbsp plain (all-purpose) flour
    (or a gluten-free flour)
4 tbsp olive oil
4 tbsp coconut oil
1 tsp sea salt
1 tsp cracked black pepper
3 sprigs of fresh rosemary
3 shallots, peeled and quartered
4 garlic cloves

Serves
6

Cooks In
55 minutes

Difficulty
2/10

**Can be GF, if GF
flour is used**

First up, preheat your oven to 180°C (350°F). Cut your potatoes into similar-sized pieces, pop them into a large saucepan filled with water and add a pinch of salt.

Cover the saucepan and place it over a high heat. Bring to the boil and cook for 4–5 minutes, or until the potatoes just start to soften on the outsides.

Tip the parboiled potatoes into a colander to drain, then return them to the saucepan to steam dry for a few minutes before sprinkling over the flour.

Place the lid back on the saucepan and give the pan a good shake for 30 seconds. This creates the rough edges on the potatoes which is key to getting crispy roasties.

Pour the oils into a deep-sided, non-stick, metal baking tray and set on your hob over a very low heat. Add the potatoes before it gets hot and allow the potatoes to colour a little bit, turning them often, for around 3 minutes. Season the potatoes with the salt and pepper, and add the rosemary, shallots and garlic to the tray.

Once the potatoes are lightly golden, transfer the tray to the oven for 35 minutes, or until the potatoes are crispy and golden. I usually turn my roasties half way through cooking.

Hasselback Potatoes with "Cheese" Sauce

Another beautiful potato dish! The beauty of the hasselback is that the flavour gets right into the potato and the slices crisp up beautifully.

500g (1lb 2oz) baby potatoes
3 tbsp olive oil
1 tbsp dried rosemary
2 tsp sea salt
1 tsp cracked black pepper
zest of 1 lemon
1 garlic clove, crushed
handful of fresh chives, chopped,
　　to serve
handful of dried cranberries,
　　to serve

For the "cheese" sauce
80g (½ cup) raw cashew nuts
120ml (scant ½ cup) filtered
　　cold water
120ml (scant ½ cup) cold
　　non-dairy milk
2 tbsp tapioca starch
3 tbsp nutritional yeast
1 tsp tahini
1 tsp white miso
pinch of sea salt and
　　white pepper

Serves
6

Cooks In
50 minutes

Difficulty
5/10

GF

First up, preheat your oven to 180°C (350°F). Next, grab yourself a wooden spoon and sit a potato in the bowl of the spoon. Starting at one end, cut across the potato width-ways at 3mm (⅛in) intervals. The spoon will stop you cutting right through the potato. Carry on until you've sliced into all the potatoes, placing them into a roasting tray as you go.

Mix together the oil, rosemary, seasoning, lemon zest and garlic in a small mixing bowl, then use a pastry brush to brush the mixture all over the potatoes, making sure you get lots into the potato cuts. Once all the potatoes are coated, bake for 30–35 minutes, or until golden.

While the potatoes are in the oven, blitz together all the "cheese" sauce ingredients in a blender until smooth, then pour into a small saucepan. Heat the sauce over a low heat, stirring constantly with a spatula, until it's thick and creamy.

When the potatoes are cooked, sprinkle over the chives and dried cranberries and serve them straight away with the sauce on the side or drizzled over the top.

Grilled Tenderstem

This is my favourite way to serve tenderstem. Make sure you get lots of nice charred marks on the broccoli, the flavour is fire!

300g (10½oz) tenderstem
    broccoli
2 tbsp olive oil
1 garlic clove, crushed
1 tbsp tamari soy sauce
pinch of cracked black pepper

Serves
4

Cooks In
15 minutes

Difficulty
2/10

GF

Bring a large saucepan of water to the boil, then drop in the broccoli and cook for 3 minutes. Meanwhile preheat a griddle pan over a high heat.

After 3 minutes of cooking, remove the broccoli from the water with a slotted spoon and pat dry with kitchen paper.

Add the oil to the griddle pan followed by the garlic – spread it around the griddle pan with a wooden spoon. Immediately add the broccoli and cook for a couple of minutes and then turn over to cook the other side. Char lines are good – they will add great flavour.

Once nicely charred, turn off the heat and add the soy sauce and pepper to give a punch of umami flavour. Stir the broccoli a couple of times, then serve.

Celeriac Purée

This is luxurious, silky and creamy. It is great served with my
Rich portobello mushroom and lentil spiral (page 83).

1 celeriac (celery root), peeled
and chopped into small cubes
480ml (scant 2 cups)
non-dairy milk
240ml (scant 1 cup)
vegetable stock
juice of 1 lemon
½ tsp sea salt
½ tsp ground white pepper
2 tbsp extra virgin olive oil

Serves
4

Cooks In
30 minutes

Difficulty
2/10

GF

Heat all the ingredients in a large saucepan over a medium heat, with the lid on, for around 15 minutes. Stir every now and then. Once the celeriac is soft, take the pan off the heat.

Let everything cool slightly before ladling it into a blender. Blitz until you have a smooth purée. You may need to do this in batches if your blender is small.

Pour the purée back into the saucepan and check it for seasoning. If it's slightly bland, add more salt, pepper and lemon juice to bring out the flavours.

Christmas Condiments

The essential condiments to spruce up your Christmas meal.

Cranberry and orange sauce
Makes 360g (13oz)

300g (3 cups) fresh cranberries
1 tsp grated fresh ginger
1 small cinnamon stick
1 Braeburn apple, grated
200g (1 cup) caster (superfine) sugar
240ml (1 cup) fresh orange juice

Heat all the ingredients in a heavy-based saucepan over a low heat with the lid on. Cook for 15 minutes, stirring often.

Spoon the sauce into your sterilized jars and seal. The sauce will keep for 4 weeks in the fridge.

> To sterilize your jars, place them in a large saucepan filled with cold water, place over a medium heat and bring to a simmer. Simmer for 3 minutes, then turn off the heat. Carefully remove the jars from the water when you're ready to fill them.

Horseradish sauce
Makes enough for one meal

5cm (2in) fresh horseradish, grated and
    soaked in boiling water for 3 minutes
150g (¾ cup) vegan mayonnaise
zest and juice of ½ lemon
1 tbsp agave nectar
pinch of sea salt and pepper

Drain the soaked horseradish and mix with the other ingredients in a small bowl. Serve the same day as making.

Mint sauce
Makes 10 servings

30g (1oz) fresh mint leaves
4 tbsp white wine vinegar
5 tbsp boiling water
1 heaped tbsp caster (superfine) sugar
pinch of salt

Finely chop the mint leaves, then place in a heatproof jug. Add the rest of the ingredients, stir together and chill for at least 2 hours. Serve within 2–3 days.

Fluffy Yorkshire Puddings

This was a hard recipe for me to crack, but after several attempts I managed to veganize Yorkshire puddings! Make sure you get your baking tin very hot for this!

vegetable oil, for greasing
260g (2 generous cups) self-raising flour
1½ tsp baking powder
1 tsp sea salt
480ml (2 cups) soy milk, or vegan milk of your choice

Makes
12

Cooks In
30 minutes

Difficulty
5/10

Preheat the oven to 210°C (420°F). Pour about 2 teaspoons of oil into each hole of a 12-hole Yorkshire-pudding baking tin.

Mix the flour, baking powder and salt together well in a large mixing bowl. Add the milk to the bowl, whisk together until smooth, then pour the batter into a jug.

Now it's time to get the baking tray hot – place it into the oven for 4 minutes, then remove the tray and quickly fill each hole with batter.

Carefully put the tray back into the oven for 16 minutes, or until the puddings are golden brown and nicely risen.

Serve straight away.

Sweet Potato and Chestnut Stuffing

Stuffing is one of my favourite parts of the Christmas dinner. I love this recipe, it has all the Christmassy flavours you could want. It tastes amazing when stuffed inside my "no-turkey" centre piece (page 68).

2 tbsp olive oil
1 leek, finely chopped
2 garlic cloves, crushed
1 tbsp dried sage
2 tsp dried rosemary
½ tsp ground cinnamon
150g (5½oz) sweet potato, peeled, cubed and steamed
95g (½ cup) dried apricots, finely chopped
45g (¼ cup) dried cranberries, finely chopped
50g (¾ cup) breadcrumbs (gluten-free if necessary)
100g (3½oz) vacuum-packed chestnuts, chopped
200g (1 cup) canned chickpeas (garbanzos) or butterbeans
zest of 1 lemon

Serves
6

Cooks In
55 minutes

Difficulty
2/10

GF

First, preheat the oven to 180°C (350°F) and then line a medium-sized baking dish with greaseproof paper.

Heat the oil in a large, non-stick frying pan over a medium heat. Add the leek, garlic, herbs, cinnamon and cooked sweet potato and sauté until the leek has softened and the potato has browned. Add all the remaining ingredients and toss until well combined. Turn the heat off and, using an old-fashioned potato masher, lightly mash the mix. Break down any large chunks of sweet potato and the chickpeas/butterbeans.

Spoon the mixture into the lined baking dish and press it in to compact the mixture.

Place the dish onto a baking tray and slide it into the oven to bake for 35–40 minutes. Once it's cooked, allow the stuffing to cool before taking it out of the dish and peeling off the paper.

If you are using this to stuff the Stuffed roasted "joint" (page 68), skip the final step.

Pan-roasted Pumpkin Wedges

Pumpkin is one of my favourite vegetables. Make sure you allow
it to caramelize until golden-brown for maximum flavour.

Ingredients	Info

1 small pumpkin or squash
3 tbsp olive oil, plus a little extra
1 tbsp miso paste
pinch of sea salt and cracked
  black pepper
3 tbsp maple syrup
12 fresh sage leaves
seeds from 1 pomegranate,
  to serve

Serves
6

Cooks In
40 minutes

Difficulty
5/10

GF

Preheat your oven to 180°C (350°F). Using a serrated knife, top and tail the pumpkin. Cut it in half down the middle and scoop out the seeds. Wash the pulp off the seeds and roast in the oven for 12 minutes, then set aside. Slice the pumpkin into 2.5-cm (1-in) thick wedges.

Bring a large saucepan of water to the boil, carefully add the pumpkin wedges and cook for 6–8 minutes, then drain into a colander, shake off any water, return to the empty saucepan and leave to steam dry and cool slightly.

Whisk together the oil and miso paste in a large mixing bowl. Add the pumpkin wedges and give them a little toss to make sure they are nicely coated. Try not to break any.

Heat a little oil in a large, non-stick frying pan over a medium heat and, when the pan is hot, fry a few wedges at a time (don't overcrowd the pan) for 3–4 minutes on each side, or until golden. Sprinkle over some salt and pepper and drizzle over a little of the maple syrup. Once golden on both sides, remove the wedges and transfer to a baking tray to keep warm in the oven. Repeat until you have fried all the wedges.

Leave the pan on the heat, add a couple of tablespoons more of oil if there's none left in the pan. Throw in the sage leaves and cook for 2 minutes until crisp. Remove the sage leaves from the pan onto a couple of sheets of kitchen paper to soak up any excess oil. Serve the pumpkin wedges with the fried sage leaves, pomegranate seeds and roasted pumpkin seeds sprinkled over the top.

ALL THE TRIMMINGS

119

Leftovers

Ultimate Xmas Burger

Build the most delicious Christmas burgers using a bunch of your dinner leftovers. These burgers are so indulgent with lashings of gravy.

1 recipe quantity Bubble and
squeak patties (page 134)
leftover Shredded mushroom
"meat" (page 58)
leftover greens (whatever you
have, or leave out)
leftover gravy
4 burger buns, toasted
Red cabbage sauerkraut
(page 177)
Cranberry and orange sauce
(page 114)
mayonnaise

Serves
4

Cooks In
25 minutes

Difficulty
3/10

Can be GF

Preheat the oven to 180°C (360°F). Put your bubble and squeak patties, mushroom meat and greens on a baking tray and pop in the oven for 20–25 minutes, or until thoroughly reheated.

Meanwhile, heat up your gravy in a saucepan or in the microwave.

Once everything is hot, build your burgers, layering up all your reheated leftovers in toasted burger buns. I add lashings of cranberry sauce, mayonnaise and gravy. Serve straight away.

Mega Chips

The Pommes Anna can be turned into the most magical mega chips. Serve them with a dip of your choice – my Brussels sprout kimchi goes so well with them.

---

1 quantity (or at least half a batch) Pommes Anna (page 90)
500ml (2 cups) vegetable oil, for frying
sea salt and pepper
Brussels sprout kimchi, (page 176), to serve
handful of thyme leaves, finely chopped, to garnish

Serves
12 (if using a whole batch of Pommes Anna)

Cooks In
20 minutes

Difficulty
7/10

GF

Turn the Pommes Anna out of its tray and carefully cut it into rectangles measuring roughly 3 x 7cm (1¼ x 2¾in).

Heat the oil in a large non-stick pan over a medium heat. When the oil is hot, gently fry a few pieces at a time for around 3–4 minutes on each side until crisp and golden.

When the potatoes are cooked, remove them from the oil and place onto a plate lined with kitchen paper. Sprinkle over a little salt and pepper and some fresh thyme, then I like to serve them with my Brussels sprout kimchi.

Leftover Christmas Pie

I don't think there's anything better than a warming pie the day after Christmas; it's the perfect way to use up any leftover veg from the big day.

2 tbsp olive oil or water
2 leeks, washed and finely chopped
2 garlic cloves, crushed
160g (¾ cup) sweetcorn
200g (7oz) leftover Stuffed roast "joint" (page 68), stuffing removed and cut into cubes (or leftover vegetables)
1 tsp sea salt
2 tsp cracked black pepper
240ml (scant 1 cup) vegan-friendly white wine or vegetable stock

360ml (1½ cups) oat or soy cream or coconut milk
1 tbsp white miso paste
a little flour, for dusting
320g (11oz) ready-made vegan puff pastry

For the glaze
4 tbsp maple syrup
4 tbsp non-dairy milk
4 tbsp vegetable oil

Serves
6

Cooks In
55 minutes

Difficulty
5/10

Can be GF, if GF pastry is used

Heat the oil or water in a large saucepan placed over a medium heat. When hot, add the leeks and garlic and sauté for 3–4 minutes until soft. Add the sweetcorn and "turkey" (or veg), stir with a wooden spoon, and cook for a further 3 minutes. A little caramelization on the turkey will add a great flavour. Add the seasoning, then pour in the wine or stock, scraping any bits off the bottom to deglaze the pan. Cook for a further 3 minutes.

Stir in the cream and miso paste and simmer gently for 15 minutes – don't let it boil. After 15 minutes, it should be nice and creamy. Check the seasoning, and add more if needed. Scrape the filling into a 23cm (9in) pie dish and leave it to cool for around 25 minutes.

Meanwhile, preheat your oven to 180°C (350°F). Lightly flour a clean work surface and roll out your pastry to around 4mm (⅛in) thick and wide enough to fit over your pie dish. Carefully transfer the pastry and lay it over the filling, gently pressing around the edges of the pie dish to seal and trim off any overhanging pastry. Pinch the pastry around the edge of the pie dish to create a fluted edge. Get creative with the pastry trimmings – roll out again and cut into festive shapes or letters to decorate your pie, brushing with milk.

Mix the glaze ingredients together in a small bowl, then brush the glaze over the pie top and decoration. Bake on the lower shelf of the preheated oven for 30 minutes until the pastry is beautiful and golden. I like to brush over a little more glaze just before serving.

Christmas Korma

I am so inspired by Indian food, especially dishes from Southern India. I dream of travelling to India one day, but for now, making delicious curries is enough. Make sure you cook the onions with the spices for the full 10 minutes to make sure they are golden and sweet. This is another amazing way of using up any leftover Christmas food.

5 tbsp vegetable oil
3 cardamom pods
2 cloves
2 fresh or frozen curry leaves
1 cinnamon stick
2 white onions, finely sliced
1 tsp sea salt
2 tsp caster (superfine) sugar
3 garlic cloves, peeled
thumb-sized piece of fresh ginger, peeled
½ tsp red chilli powder (add more if you like a kick)
½ tsp ground fenugreek
2 tsp ground cumin
1 tsp turmeric
2 tsp ground coriander
¼ tsp ground nutmeg
200g (7oz) leftover "turkey" (page 68) or "beef" (page 74), cut into chunks (optional)

2 sweet potatoes, peeled and cubed
400g (14oz) can of chickpeas (garbanzos), drained
25g (¼ cup) dried cranberries
3 tbsp coconut flour
400ml (14fl oz) can of full-fat coconut milk
240ml (scant 1 cup) vegetable stock

To serve
2 tomatoes, cut into chunks
1 red onion, finely chopped
handful of fresh coriander (cilantro), finely chopped
juice of 1 lime
1 small green chilli, finely chopped
lime wedges
handful of dried cranberries

Method overleaf...

Serves
6

Cooks In
60 minutes

Difficulty
5/10

Can be GF, if "turkey" and "beef" are left out

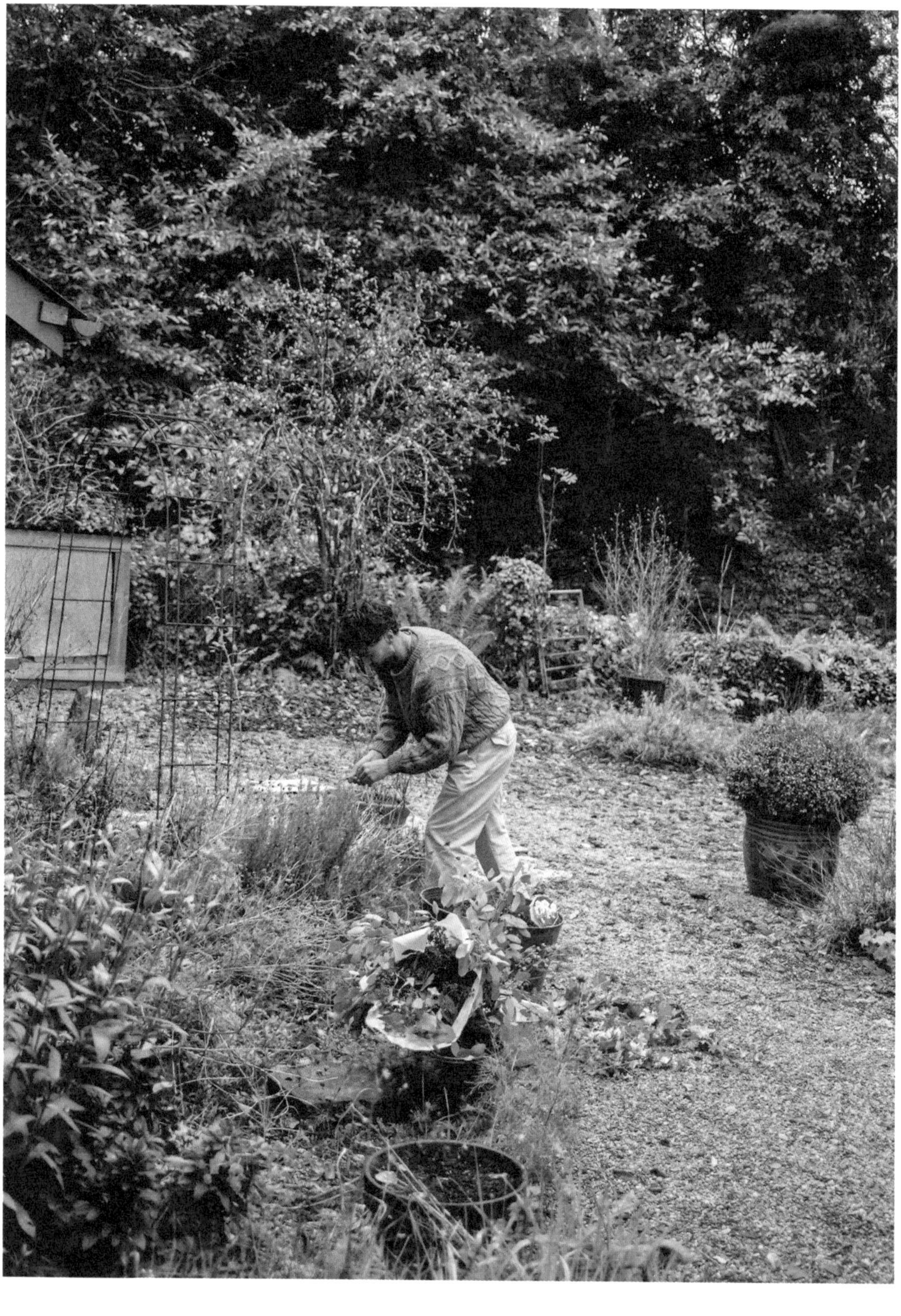

Christmas korma continued...

Heat a large saucepan over a medium heat, add the oil followed by the cardamom pods, cloves, curry leaves and cinnamon stick. Cook for 2 minutes, then add the onions with the sea salt and sugar and stir constantly, cooking the onions for 8 minutes until golden and crisp but not burnt.

Put the garlic and ginger and a tablespoon of water into a blender and blitz until smooth. Add this paste to the crisp onions in the pan, cook for 1 minute, then add the spices. Cook for 4 minutes, stirring often.

Add the "meat", if using, the sweet potatoes, the chickpeas and the cranberries. Continue to stir and cook for 4 more minutes.

Sprinkle in the coconut flour and stir well to mix it in, then add the coconut milk and stock. Give everything a good stir and turn the heat down low. Allow the curry to simmer away for 25 minutes, stirring every now and then, until the curry is thick and creamy.

To make a side salad, simply mix together the tomato, red onion, coriander (cilantro), lime juice and chilli. Serve alongside the curry with extra lime wedges and a sprinkling of cranberries.

Gyros

Who says the party has to stop after Christmas Day? These delicious kebabs are perfect party food. Use leftover "beef" cut into fine strips and seasoned up. Incredible!

For the "meat"
200g (7oz) slow-roast "beef" (page 74), shredded
1 tsp smoked paprika
¼ tsp cayenne pepper
½ tsp ground cumin
½ tsp ground coriander
½ tsp dried garlic powder
2 tsp dried mixed herbs
pinch of sea salt and pepper
3 tbsp vegetable oil

For the mint yogurt
285g (generous 1 cup) dairy-free plain yogurt
handful of fresh mint leaves, finely chopped
7.5cm (3in) piece of cucumber, deseeded and finely chopped

1 garlic clove, crushed
½ tsp paprika
1 tsp sea salt
juice of ½ lemon
2 tbsp extra virgin olive oil (optional)

For the salad
2 baby gem lettuces, shredded
2 medium tomatoes, sliced
½ red onion, finely sliced
handful of fresh coriander (cilantro)
4–6 pickled chillies, from a jar

To serve
toasted pitta bread or flat breads
hot sauce
lemon wedges

Serves
4

Cooks In
40 minutes

Difficulty
5/10

First up, mix all the ingredients for the "meat" together in a large mixing bowl. Cover and set aside to allow the flavours to mingle.

Meanwhile, put all the ingredients for the mint yogurt in a mixing bowl and stir well to combine. Cover with cling film (plastic wrap) and chill in the fridge until you're ready to serve.

Heat a large, non-stick pan over a high heat, then add the "meat" and cook for 4–5 minutes. Stir often and try and get lots of colour on the "meat".

To serve, fill your pitta breads or flat breads with generous amounts of the "meat", the various salad elements and a dollop of mint yogurt. A drizzle of hot sauce adds a nice kick and a squeeze of lemon juice brings all the flavours together.

Bubble and Squeak Patties

You can use whatever leftovers you have for bubble and squeak. This is a basic guide to using up some of the dishes from the previous chapters. My tip for the perfect bubble and squeak is to make sure you have plenty of potatoes – these will help bind all the leftovers together – so when you cook roasties, make more than you need so you have enough left over!

5–6 leftover Roasties (page 109)
2–3 leftover Orange-glazed carrots (page 106)
handful of Braised red cabbage (page 102)
8–10 Sexy sprouts (page 105)
4–5 Sticky beetroot (page 102)
3–4 Maple pan-roasted parsnips (page 104)
4–5 stems of Grilled tenderstem broccoli (page 112)
handful of fresh parsley, stems included
handful of chopped "meat" (leftovers from any of the "meat" recipes)

4–5 tbsp plain (all-purpose) flour, plus extra for dusting
zest of 1 lemon
2 tbsp Cranberry and orange sauce (page 114)
4 tbsp Rich white wine gravy (page 71)
3–4 tbsp olive oil, for frying

To serve
1 avocado
mixed leaf salad

Serves
6

Cooks In
45 minutes

Difficulty
5/10

Nut roast can be a nice addition

Preheat the oven to 180°C (350°F) and line a baking tray with greaseproof paper. First up, mash up the roasties in a mixing bowl using an old-fashioned potato masher.

Put the other vegetables and the parsley into a blender and pulse until the vegetables are all a similar size. Add these to the bowl of potato, followed by the chopped "meat", then mix everything together thoroughly. Stir in the flour, lemon zest, cranberry sauce and gravy.

Lightly flour your hands and the lined baking tray. Divide the mixture into four and use your hands to form into individual patties, approximately burger-sized.

Heat the oil in a non-stick frying pan over a medium heat and add a couple of patties. Cook for 3–4 minutes on each side until golden, then carefully remove them from the pan and place them into the lined baking tray. Continue with the remaining patties. Pop the tray into the preheated oven and bake the patties for 12 minutes. Serve straight away, simply with avocado and salad leaves.

LEFTOVERS

Sweet Chilli, Crispy "Beef" Stir fry

Another great way to use up leftover "beef", playing on Asian flavours. The beef strips get super crispy when fried. Use any combination of leftover vegetables that you fancy.

For the sweet chilli sauce
250ml (1 cup) filtered water
125ml (½ cup) white wine vinegar
125ml (½ cup) tomato purée (paste)
2 tbsp Sriracha
1 tbsp sweet chilli flakes (or hot, if you prefer)
3 tbsp caster (superfine) sugar

For the crispy "beef"
500ml (2 cups) vegetable oil, for frying
125g (1 cup) cornflour (cornstarch)
1 tsp sea salt
250ml (1 cup) ice-cold sparkling water
200g (7oz) leftover "beef" (page 74), cut into thin strips, or shredded mushroom "meat" (page 58)

For the stir-fry veg
2 tbsp sesame oil
4 leftover Orange-glazed carrots (page 106), evenly chopped
4–5 leftover Grilled tenderstem (page 112), evenly chopped
1 red onion, finely sliced
2 baby pak choi (bok choy), quartered

To serve
rice or noodles
toasted sesame seeds
handful of fresh coriander (cilantro) leaves

Serves
4

Cooks In
45 minutes

Difficulty
5/10

First up, prepare the sweet chilli sauce – add everything to a small saucepan and whisk until combined. Place over a very low heat and let the sauce simmer away for 15 minutes to gradually thicken up. Stir from time to time.

Heat the vegetable oil in a wok or large saucepan, making sure the oil doesn't come up higher than half way. Alternatively, use a deep-fat fryer set at 180°C (350°F).

Mix the cornflour, salt and sparkling water together in a bowl to form the batter.

Test if the oil is hot enough to fry the crispy beef – place a cube of bread into the oil and if it bubbles and floats to the surface, your oil is ready.

Coat a few strips of "beef" in the batter, and make sure they are well covered. Lower the coated strips carefully into the oil a few at a time. Try not to drop them together in one clump as they will stick together. Fry the strips for 3–4 minutes until crisp. Once golden, lift out of the oil with a slotted spoon onto a plate lined with kitchen paper to absorb any excess oil. Fry the rest of the "beef", then set aside while you quickly stir fry the vegetables.

Recipe continues overleaf...

Sweet chilli, crispy "beef" stir fry continues...

Heat a large, non-stick frying pan over a high heat. Add the sesame oil, followed by the vegetables and stir fry for 3–4 minutes. If you're using fresh vegetables, you may need to cook them for slightly longer. When the vegetables have lightly browned, add the crispy "beef" strips followed by a couple of ladles of sweet chilli sauce. Toss the pan to make sure everything is coated in the sauce and serve immediately with rice or noodles, toasted sesame seeds and fresh coriander.

Zesty, Warm Salad

Something a little lighter, after maybe over-indulging on Christmas Day! This salad is a great zesty pick-me-up.

200g (7oz) cavolo nero or curly kale, stems removed, roughly chopped
180g (1 cup) wild rice, cooked and chilled
180g (1 cup) quinoa, cooked and chilled
4 tbsp mixed seeds (pumpkin, sesame, linseed, sunflower)
75g (½ cup) walnuts, crushed
50g (½ cup) dried cranberries, chopped
juice of 2 lemons
handful of fresh basil leaves, chopped
5 tbsp extra virgin olive oil
3 tbsp balsamic vinegar

1 tsp sea salt
1 tsp cracked black pepper
5–6 Pan-roasted pumpkin wedges (page 119), cubed (optional)

To serve
2 blood oranges, peeled and segmented

Serves
4

Cooks In
20 minutes

Difficulty
2/10

GF

Bring a large saucepan of water to the boil, add the cavolo nero or kale and blanch for 2 minutes before draining into a colander. Let the leaves cool slightly.

Put the rest of the salad ingredients into a large mixing bowl and stir well to combine everything. Once the cavolo nero or kale leaves have cooled, fold them through the rest of the salad.

Serve the salad straight away with the orange segments.

Afters

Ginger-nut Pumpkin Pie with Torched Meringue

My take on a classic pumpkin pie, this is nothing short of a show stopper – an incredible holiday treat.

175g (6oz) ginger nut biscuits
   (ginger cookies)
175g (6oz) mixed nuts
185g (¾ cup) plant butter, melted

For the filling
1 medium pumpkin or squash (around
   2kg/4lb 8oz in weight)
3 tbsp olive oil
125ml (½ cup) maple syrup
400ml (14fl oz) can of full-fat coconut milk
60g (scant ½ cup) plain (all-purpose) flour

55g (½ cup) cornflour (cornstarch)
½ tsp ground nutmeg
½ tsp ground ginger
½ tsp ground cinnamon
2 tsp vanilla bean paste

For the meringue
125ml (½ cup) aquafaba (liquid from
   a can of chickpeas)
½ tsp cream of tartar
55g (scant ½ cup) icing (confectioner's) sugar
1 tsp vanilla extract

Serves
8

Cooks In
2 hours

Difficulty
7/10

Preheat your oven to 180ºC (350ºF). Cut the pumpkin or squash in half and scoop out the seeds. Place it, cut side up, on a baking tray, drizzle over the oil and roast for 1 hour, or until the flesh is tender. Once cooked, spoon out the flesh and add it to your food processor, along with the maple syrup, coconut milk, flour, cornflour, spices and vanilla. Blend until the mix is super smooth.

Set the filling aside and clean the food processor bowl. Add the biscuits and nuts to the bowl, then blitz until you have a fine breadcrumb-like consistency. Add the melted butter and pulse a couple more times to combine.

Transfer the biscuit mixture to a 20–23cm (8–9in) pie tin – I use a loose-bottomed one to make the pie easy to remove after baking. Press the crumb into the tin really well, building it up the sides and into all the corners.

Place the tin into the oven to pre-cook the base for 8 minutes. When the base is a little golden, remove it from the oven and let it cool and set for 10 minutes or so.

Pour the filling into the cooled pie shell, then bake the pumpkin pie for 30 minutes, or until the edges of the filling colour and set. Turn the oven off but leave the pie in there for a further 30 minutes – the residual heat will gently cook the pie through. When the pie is cooked, remove it from the oven and leave to cool completely.

When you're ready to serve, add all the meringue ingredients to a mixing bowl and, using a hand whisk, whisk until you have stiff peaks.

Spoon the meringue on top of the pie and serve up. If you have a blow torch, you can toast the meringue on top.

Sticky Toffee Pudding with Miso Caramel Sauce

A classic dessert that has stood the test of time.
I like to use rich miso to slightly salt the caramel sauce.

½ ripe banana
240ml (1 cup) non-dairy milk
100g (scant ½ cup) plant butter, plus extra
    for greasing
220g (⅔ cup) maple syrup
100g (½ cup) brown sugar
225g (1¾ cups) self-raising flour, plus extra
    for dusting
1 tsp bicarbonate of soda (baking soda)
1 tbsp mixed spice
10 dates, finely chopped and soaked in 125ml
    (½ cup) boiling water

ice cream, to serve
chopped pistachio nuts, to serve (optional)

For the miso caramel sauce
200g (1 cup) coconut sugar
4 tbsp maple syrup
120ml (½ cup) non-dairy milk
115g (½ cup) plant butter
1 tsp vanilla bean paste
2 tsp miso paste

Serves
6

Cooks In
90 minutes

Difficulty
5/10

Can be GF

Preheat your oven to 180ºC (350ºF). Grease and flour 6 mini pudding tins (each about 200ml/¾ cup) and place them into a deep baking dish or tray.

In a mixing bowl, mash together the banana and milk until there's hardly any lumps.

In another large bowl, beat together the plant butter, maple syrup and brown sugar until the sugar has dissolved. Sift in the flour, bicarbonate of soda and mixed spice, then fold until fully incorporated. Drain the dates and stir them into the batter, along with the banana and milk mixture.

Spoon the mixture into your pudding tins, leaving around a 1.5cm (½in) gap for the puddings to rise. Pour boiling water into the baking dish, to come three-quarters of the way up the pudding tins, and cover the tray with foil. Place the puddings in the oven to bake for 45 minutes.

Meanwhile, make the miso caramel sauce. Add the coconut sugar and maple syrup to a heavy based saucepan. Place the pan over a medium heat and allow the sugar to melt to an amber coloured caramel. Once melted, take the saucepan off the heat and carefully whisk in the milk and plant butter. Once incorporated and saucy, place the sauce back over a low heat and add the vanilla and miso.

After 45 minutes of baking, test the puddings are cooked by inserting a skewer into the middle of them – if the skewer comes out clean, they are ready. Let the puddings sit for about 5 minutes before turning them out of the tins.

Serve the puddings with the caramel sauce, ice cream and a sprinkling of pistachios, if you like.

AFTERS

Cranberry Bakewell Tart

Rather than using traditional cherries, I use Christmassy cranberries for this Bakewell tart. It stores really well, so can be enjoyed a few days after Christmas.

1 recipe sweet pastry (page 155), or
    shop-bought short-crust pastry
plain (all-purpose) flour, for dusting
240g (1 cup) cranberry sauce
50g (½ cup) flaked (sliced) almonds

For the almond "frangipane" layer
120ml (½ cup) aquafaba (liquid from
    a can of chickpeas)
6 tbsp icing (confectioner's) sugar
170g (¾ cup) plant butter

220g (heaped ½ cup) caster (superfine) sugar
160g (scant 1 cup) ground almonds
2 tbsp vanilla bean paste
3 tbsp almond extract
100g plain (all-purpose) flour
4 tbsp cornflour (cornstarch)

For the icing (optional)
60g (½ cup) icing (confectioner's) sugar
1 tsp vanilla extract

Serves
10

Cooks In
90 minutes

Difficulty
9/10

Follow the instructions on page 155 to prepare the sweet pastry and chill in the freezer for 25 minutes. Meanwhile, preheat your oven to 180ºC (360ºF) and grease a 23cm (9in) loose-bottomed tart pan.

Remove your pastry from the fridge and roll it out on a sheet of lightly floured greaseproof paper to around 3mm (⅛in) thick. Carefully pick up the pastry using the greaseproof paper then turn it out into the tart pan. Don't worry, it doesn't have to be perfect; if your pastry splits or breaks, just fill any holes with excess pastry dough, then trim off any pastry that's over hanging the edges.

Place a circle of greaseproof paper on top of the pastry and weigh it down with a large handful of dried beans or rice. Place the tart case into the oven for 10 minutes, then carefully remove the beans and paper and cook for a further 6 minutes. Remove it from the oven and set it aside to cool. Do not remove it from the tart pan just yet.

Meanwhile, make the frangipane. Add the chickpea water to a large bowl along with the icing sugar and whisk until it resembles stiff peaks, like an Italian meringue.

In another bowl, whisk the butter and sugar together until light and creamy. Fold in the rest of the frangipane ingredients using a rubber spatula, then add the meringue gradually. Transfer the frangipane to a piping bag, then place the bag in the fridge for 5 minutes to cool.

Once the pastry base has cooled, spoon in the cranberry sauce and spread out evenly. Pipe the frangipane mix evenly over the top. Sprinkle the flaked almonds over the frangipane, then place the tart in the oven for 20 minutes or until the almonds on top are golden.

Meanwhile, if you want to add icing, whisk the icing sugar with 4 tablespoons of water and the vanilla until smooth. Allow the tart to cool completely before slicing and serving with the icing drizzled over the top.

Tiramisu

Making this Italian classic plant-based was surprisingly easy. It's the perfect festive dessert and even more show stopping when you serve it with a sparkler!

For the sponge
250ml (1 cup) almond milk
1 tbsp apple cider vinegar
1 tsp vanilla bean paste
50g (¼ cup) plant butter
215g (1¾ cups) self-raising flour
(or gluten-free flour)
230g (generous 1 cup) unrefined caster
(superfine) sugar
pinch of sea salt

For the cream
2 x 400g (14oz) cans of coconut cream
170g (6oz) vegan cream cheese
1 tbsp cacao powder
3 tbsp icing (confectioner's) sugar
120ml (½ cup) good-quality coffee,
brewed over ice, or to taste
4 tbsp rum, or to taste

Toppings
grated dark chocolate
coffee beans

Serves
6

Cooks In
60 minutes

Difficulty
5/10

**Can be GF, if GF
flour is used**

Preheat your oven to 180°C (350°F) and line a 5cm (2in) deep 20 x 30cm (8 x 12in) baking tray with non-stick baking paper.

First up, the sponge! Put the almond milk, apple cider vinegar, vanilla paste and plant butter into a small saucepan over a low heat. Measure the flour, sugar and salt into a large mixing bowl. When the spread has melted, pour the milk mixture into the dry ingredients and fold together. Scrape the batter into your lined baking tray and level out.

Place the tray into the oven to bake for 12–15 minutes, or until golden and springy to the touch, then turn out the sponge onto a wire rack to cool completely.

Whisk the coconut cream, cream cheese, cacao powder and icing sugar together in a large mixing bowl until fully incorporated. Add a few tablespoons of the coffee and the rum, then taste. Adjust the flavours according to how you like it.

Cut 12 discs of sponge to fit into your serving glasses. Pop a sponge disc in the base of each glass, then a spoonful of the cream, then another sponge disc. Drizzle in a little more coffee and spoon in another layer of cream. Top each tiramisu with chocolate shavings and a couple of coffee beans. Eat straight away or chill in the fridge for up to one day.

AFTERS

Christmas Pudding

The ultimate vegan Christmas pudding – boozy, fruity and moreish!

100g (¾ cup) sultanas
100g (generous ½ cup) dried mixed peel
100g (generous ½ cup) chopped dates
50g (¼ cup) dried cherries
25g (1oz) crystallized ginger, chopped
120ml (½ cup) rum or brandy, plus extra
    brandy to serve
juice of 1 orange
zest and juice of 1 lemon
1 bay leaf
1 tsp ground nutmeg

1 tsp ground mixed spice
1 tsp ground cinnamon
½ tsp sea salt
75g (⅓ cup) demerara or coconut sugar
2 tbsp black treacle (molasses)
1 Braeburn apple, grated
115g (scant ½ cup) plant butter,
    plus extra for greasing
45g (½ cup) breadcrumbs
95g (¾ cup) plain (all-purpose) flour
½ tsp baking powder

Serves
6

Cooks In
7 hours

Difficulty
7/10

The day before, put the dried fruit plus the ginger, alcohol, orange and lemon juice and the bay leaf into a large bowl. Stir well to mix, cover and leave for at least 12 hours to plump up.

The next day, grease a 1-litre (2-pint) pudding bowl with plant butter, then line the base with a circle of greaseproof paper to ensure the pudding comes out once cooked.

Remove the bay leaf from the fruit. Add the lemon zest, spices, salt, sugar, treacle and apple and mix. Stir in the plant butter and breadcrumbs. Sift in the flour and baking powder and fold in. Spoon the mixture into the pudding bowl, leaving a 2.5cm (1in) gap at the top. Cover with greaseproof paper, then a sheet of foil and tie with cook's string.

Put an upturned ramekin in the bottom of a saucepan. Sit the pudding on top, then pour in boiling water half way up the sides of the pudding. Cover and simmer over a low heat for 5 hours, topping up the water when needed. Lift the pudding out and leave to cool.

Store for up to a month before serving. Steam again in the same way for 30 minutes. Add 2 shots of vegan-friendly brandy to a saucepan and heat over a low heat for 2 minutes. Light the brandy with a match, then carefully pour over the pudding for that festive flame.

Cinnamon-spiced Apple Crumble

This is a great dessert option if you're looking for something slightly healthier. It's gluten free and refined-sugar free but still divine.

5 crisp eating apples (such as Braeburn)
100g (scant ½ cup) coconut sugar
2 tbsp coconut oil
1 tsp vanilla bean paste or 1 vanilla pod
2 tsp ground cinnamon

For the topping
75g (scant ½ cup) rice flour
75g (¾ cup) almond flour (or coconut flour if nut-free)
pinch of sea salt

115g (½ cup) plant butter
100g (scant ½ cup) coconut sugar
45g (½ cup) gluten-free porridge oats

To serve
vegan ice cream or custard
a few sprigs of fresh mint

Serves
4

Cooks In
40 minutes

Difficulty
2/10

GF

Preheat your oven to 180°C (350°F). Core the apples, then cut three of them into 1cm (⅓in) cubes and grate the other two. Leave the skin on as that's where the best flavour is!

Put the coconut sugar into a large saucepan placed over a medium heat and wait for the sugar to melt down. Keep an eye on it to make sure it doesn't burn; it should only take 2 minutes. Add the coconut oil followed by the grated apple and cook for a couple of minutes for the apple to almost melt down.

Stir in the vanilla pod and seeds and the cinnamon and cook for 1 more minute while stirring, then add the cubed apple. Turn the heat down to its lowest setting, pop the lid on and cook for 15 minutes, stirring every now and then. Remove the vanilla pod.

Meanwhile prepare your topping. Put the rice flour, almond flour and sea salt into a large mixing bowl and stir to combine. Add the plant butter and use your fingers to rub together until it starts to become like breadcrumbs. Stir in the sugar and the oats.

Once the apples have softened, pour the filling into an 8cm (3in) deep 23cm (9in) baking dish. Cover with the crumble topping, then bake in the oven for 15 minutes, or until the crumble is golden. Serve with vegan ice cream or custard, garnished with a sprig of mint.

Crème Brûlée
Tartlets

Another classic dish that I was so pleased to veganize. Turning it into a tart was a total winner! The filling is so creamy, perfect with the crisp pastry.

For the sweet pastry (or use shop-bought short-crust pastry)
250g (2 cups) plain (all-purpose) flour
125g (1 cup) icing (confectioner's) sugar
pinch of salt
pinch of ground cinnamon
125g (½ cup) plant butter
about 2 tbsp almond milk

For the glaze
3 tbsp maple syrup
2 tbsp vegetable oil

For the crème brûlée filling
400ml (14fl oz) can of coconut milk
1 vanilla pod, seeds scraped out
300ml (1¼ cups) almond milk
4 tbsp cornflour (cornstarch)
4 tbsp icing (confectioner's) sugar
6 tbsp caster (superfine) sugar, to finish

Makes
6 tartlets

Cooks In
60 minutes

Difficulty
7/10

If you're not using pastry, you can make these traditionally in ramekins

Combine the flour, sugar, salt and cinnamon together in a mixing bowl. Add the plant butter and rub into the dry ingredients with your fingers until the mix is a breadcrumb-like consistency.

Pour in enough milk to bring the mixture together to form a ball of dough and pick up all the bits from the bowl. Give it a slight knead for 2 minutes, then wrap the dough in cling film (plastic wrap) and pop it into the freezer to chill for 25 minutes.

Preheat your oven to 180°C (350°F) and grease 6 loose-bottomed 10cm (4in) tartlet tins. Remove your pastry from the freezer and roll it out to about 3mm (⅛in) onto a sheet of greaseproof paper (which makes it easier when lifting into the tart tins). Line the tins with the pastry, gently pressing into the corners and fluted edges, and trim off any excess over-hanging. Cut 6 circles of greaseproof paper to sit over the pastry cases and fill with baking beans.

Put the tins onto a baking sheet, transfer to the oven to blind bake the pastry for 6 minutes, then remove the beans and paper and cook for a further 6 minutes, or until golden.

Remove the tartlets from the oven. Mix together the glaze ingredients in a small bowl and brush the glaze over the pastry cases. Pop the tartlets back into the oven for 3 minutes. The glaze will stop the pastry going soggy when the filling goes in. After 3 minutes, remove from the oven and leave to cool in the tins for 5 minutes before carefully removing and cooling on a wire rack.

To make the crème brûlée filling, heat the coconut milk in a saucepan with the vanilla pod and seeds over a low heat.

Recipe continues overleaf...

AFTERS

Crème brûlée tartlets continued...

Meanwhile, pour the almond milk into a bowl and whisk in the cornflour and sugar. Pour this into the heating coconut milk and whisk over a low heat until the mixture has thickened. This should take around 4 minutes. Remove the vanilla pod.

Carefully pour the custard into your tart cases. Cover each tartlet with cling film, placing the cling film directly onto the custard to stop a skin forming, then chill in the fridge for at least an hour to set, or until you're ready to serve.

Before serving, remove the cling film and sprinkle a tablespoon of caster sugar over each tartlet. Caramelize the sugar using a blow torch or place the tarts under a hot grill for around 4 minutes.

AFTERS

Spiced Hot Chocolate

The best hot chocolate ever!

1 litre (4 cups) non-dairy milk
4 tbsp cacao powder
1 tsp vanilla bean paste
¼ tsp ground ginger
¼ tsp ground cinnamon
4 tbsp maple syrup
100g (3½oz) dairy-free
    chocolate, grated

To serve
2 tsp cacao powder
vegan marshmallows (optional)

Serves

4

Cooks In

25 minutes

Difficulty

2/10

GF

Heat all the ingredients for the hot chocolate (except the grated chocolate) together in a saucepan until it reaches a light simmer, then add the chocolate. Whisk until the chocolate has melted – don't let it boil.

Serve your hot chocolate in mugs, topped with a sprinkle of cacao powder and vegan marshmallows, if you like.

Grilled Mango and Coconut Panna Cotta

A more tropical-inspired Christmas dessert because, of course, not all countries are cold at Christmas! I recommend using 5cm (2½in) stainless steel dariole moulds or plastic mini jelly moulds.

400ml (14fl oz) can of full-fat coconut milk
1 shot vegan-friendly rum, optional
1 vanilla pod, seeds scraped out (or 2 tsp vanilla bean paste)
250ml (1 cup) non-dairy milk
65g (½ cup) cornflour (cornstarch)
5 tbsp coconut honey or maple syrup

For the mango dressing
200g (7oz) mango, peeled and cubed
120ml (½ cup) water
½ tsp dried chilli flakes

For the grilled mango
1 tbsp coconut oil, plus extra for greasing
½ mango, peeled and cut into 2.5cm (1in) thick slices
2 tbsp coconut sugar

To serve
fresh mint leaves, chopped
coconut flakes, lightly toasted

Makes
6

Cooks In
60 minutes

Difficulty
5/10

GF

Lightly grease 6 moulds with coconut oil and place on a baking tray. Heat the coconut milk and rum in a saucepan over a low heat. Add the vanilla pod and seeds. Allow to infuse while you whisk the non-dairy milk, cornflour and coconut honey together in a bowl until smooth. Scrape the cornflour mixture into the saucepan and stir until it has thickened up, about 4–5 minutes.

Remove from the heat, remove the vanilla pod and spoon the mix into your moulds. Tap them on the surface to level out. Cover with cling film (plastic wrap) and refrigerate for at least 3 hours.

Blitz the dressing ingredients in a blender until smooth. If the dressing is too thick, add more water.

Before serving, heat a griddle pan over a high heat. Melt the coconut oil, then add the mango slices and griddle until lightly charred, then sprinkle over the coconut sugar for additional caramelization. Griddle the mango on all sides for around 3–4 minutes.

To turn the panna cotta out of their moulds, simply dip the base of each mould into hot water to loosen them, then invert onto a serving plate. Serve with the grilled mango and plenty of dressing, sprinkled with mint and coconut flakes.

Chocolate Orange Raw "Cheesecake"

Another showstopper... a creamy "cheesecake". This is sweetened with natural sugar and is totally raw. Chocolate orange – the taste of Christmas.

For the base
170g (1⅔ cups) ground almonds
80g (½ cup) macadamia nuts
40g (½ cup) pecans
3 tbsp agave nectar
3 tbsp coconut oil
1 tbsp peanut butter
pinch of sea salt

For the filling
340g (2½ cups) raw cashew nuts, soaked for
    at least 1 hour
240ml (1 cup) coconut oil, melted
240ml (1 cup) almond milk
400ml (14fl oz) can of coconut milk

8 tbsp maple syrup or agave nectar
2 tsp vanilla extract
2 tbsp organic cacao powder (for the
    chocolate layer)
juice and zest of 1 orange (for the
    orange layer)

For the chocolate drizzle
5 tbsp coconut oil, melted
4 tbsp organic cacao powder
2 tbsp agave nectar

Topping suggestions
fresh or dried orange slices, physalis,
    pecans, fresh mint leaves

Serves
6–8

Cooks In
**45 minutes +
setting time**

Difficulty
5/10

GF

Line a 23cm (9in) loose-bottomed cake tin with greaseproof paper. Add all the base ingredients to a blender and blitz until smooth. Spoon into the tin to form a 1cm (½in) base, pressing into the tin until compact. Freeze. Alternatively, use small individual moulds.

Put half of the filling ingredients in your blender with the 2 tablespoons of cacao powder and blitz until super-smooth to make the chocolate layer. Pour this into your chilled tin, on top of the base, and return to the freezer for at least 45 minutes to set.

Wash out your blender, then add the remaining half of the filling ingredients together with the orange juice and zest to make the orange layer. Blitz until smooth.

Remove the tin from the freezer and pour over the orange filling. Make sure it is smooth and level, then place the "cheesecake" carefully back into the freezer to set fully for at least 3 hours.

Remove the "cheesecake" from the freezer 20 minutes before serving. Pour boiling water over a tea (dish) towel, wait until you can handle it, then lay it around the cake tin for a few seconds to melt the edges – you can then release the "cheesecake" from the tin easily.

Mix together the drizzle ingredients in a bowl with a fork until smooth. Drizzle around the edge of the "cheesecake", then decorate with orange, physalis, pecans and mint.

Fried Doughnut Profiteroles

Why not combine two big desserts – doughnuts and profiteroles?

For the doughnut profiteroles
120ml (½ cup) almond milk
5 tbsp plant butter
250g (2 cups) plain (all-purpose) flour, plus extra for dusting
2 tsp baking powder
pinch of sea salt
50g (scant ½ cup) icing (confectioner's) sugar
1.5 litres (6⅓ cups) vegetable oil, for frying

For the cream filling
320ml (1⅓ cups) coconut cream
1 shot Baileys Almande or vegan liqueur (optional)

1 tsp vanilla bean paste
2 tbsp icing (confectioner's) sugar

For the chocolate sauce
300ml (1¼ cups) almond milk
3 tbsp agave nectar
100g (3½oz) dairy-free dark chocolate, finely chopped

For the sugar string
200g (1 cup) caster (superfine) sugar

Serves
4–6

Cooks In
60 minutes

Difficulty
7/10

First up, make the doughnut profiteroles. Put the milk and plant butter in a small saucepan over a low heat to melt and mix together.

Combine all the dry ingredients in a mixing bowl, then pour in the melted butter and milk and mix with a spatula until it forms a wet dough. Lightly flour your hands and your work surface. Pick up around 2 tablespoons of dough at a time and roll it in your hands to form neat balls.

Line a baking tray with kitchen paper and preheat a deep-fat fryer to 170°C (340°F), or half-fill a large saucepan with the vegetable oil and set over a medium heat. Test if it's hot enough by dropping in a little piece of dough – if it bubbles and floats to the surface, the oil is ready.

Fry 3 to 4 balls at a time for 3–4 minutes, or until golden brown. You may need to flip them over half way through cooking. When cooked, lift them out of the oil using a spider or slotted spoon, gently shaking off any excess oil, and transfer the profiteroles straight onto the lined tray, then set aside to cool.

To make the cream filling, put all the ingredients in a mixing bowl and whisk together until thick and creamy. Set aside until you're ready to serve.

Recipe continues overleaf...

Fried doughnut profiteroles continued...

To make the chocolate sauce, pour the milk and agave nectar into a saucepan and place over a low heat to warm gradually. Meanwhile, tip the chopped chocolate into a mixing bowl. When the milk is piping hot, pour it over the chocolate and stir until smooth and all the chocolate has melted.

Cut the profiteroles in half lengthways. Pipe or spoon generous amounts of the cream onto the bottom halves and stick the tops back on.

Before serving, melt the caster (superfine) sugar in a heavy-based pan until golden.

Stack your profiteroles on a serving plate, then drizzle over the chocolate sauce. Finally, using a spoon, spin the melted sugar around the stack. Be extremely careful as the sugar will be super hot.

AFTERS

A Morning-after Pick-me-up

If you need a helping hand after an indulgent
Christmas day, this is the perfect drink for you.

---

2 wedges of watermelon
2 cucumbers
2 celery sticks
2 handfuls of kale
2 handfuls of spinach
thumb-sized piece of fresh ginger
1 kiwi
1 apple

Serves
2–4

Prep Time
10 minutes

Difficulty
2/10

Cut the watermelon down into pieces so it will fit into
your juicer. Add all the ingredients to the juicer and juice.

Serve with ice and enjoy a blast of energy after drinking!

"Cheese" & Pâté Board

It wouldn't be Christmas without the cheeseboard and why can't us vegans have one too? These are indulgent "cheeses" that will really impress.

Truffle cream "cheese"
Makes 10 servings

150g (1 cup) raw cashew nuts
120ml (½ cup) water
2 tbsp nutritional yeast flakes
1 tbsp fresh lemon juice
pinch of sea salt and white pepper
2 tbsp truffle oil, or to taste

First up, you want to quick-soak the cashews in boiling water for 15 minutes. Drain the water from the nuts, put them into a blender with all the other ingredients and blitz for 15 seconds. Stir with a spatula, then blend again until smooth.

The smoother the better, so add a little more water if it needs it. Once smooth, place it into a sealed container for up to 3 days or until you're ready to serve.

Pistachio and cranberry "cheese" log
Makes 2 logs

150g (1 cup) raw cashew nuts
150g (1 cup) macadamia nuts
1 tsp dried garlic
240ml (1 cup) filtered water
zest and juice of 1 lemon
3 tbsp nutritional yeast
1 tsp white miso paste
1 tsp sea salt
5 tbsp chopped pistachios
3 tbsp chopped dried cranberries

Quick-soak the cashews and macadamias in boiling water for 15 minutes. Drain off the water and tip the nuts into the blender with the garlic, water, lemon, yeast, miso and salt. Blitz until smooth – you may need to scrape the sides a couple of times. If needed, add a touch more water. Lay a sheet of muslin (cheesecloth) inside a sieve set over a bowl. Spoon the "cheese" mixture into the muslin and tie the corners together. Twist the muslin a little to squeeze the "cheese" and start draining the water. Transfer to the fridge for at least 24 hours to let all the water drip out.

Lay a piece of cling film (plastic wrap) on your work surface, then scatter with the pistachios and cranberries. Spoon half of the drained "cheese" into the centre of the cling film. Roll up, then twist each end tightly. Repeat with the second log. Place in the freezer for 2 hours to set before serving.

Lemon and dill "cheese"
Makes 6–8 servings

a little coconut oil, for greasing
90g (¾ cup) cashews
180ml (¾ cup) boiled water
240ml (scant 1 cup) soy milk
2 tbsp tapioca starch
2 tbsp nutritional yeast
zest of ½ lemon, plus extra for serving
2 tsp dried dill, plus extra for serving
1 tbsp lemon juice
2 tbsp agar agar powder
pinch of sea salt and white pepper

Grease two 9cm (3½in) moulds or containers with a little coconut oil – I like little round "cheeses" so I use small cake tins or ramekins.

Quick-soak the nuts in boiling water for 15 minutes. Once the nuts have softened, drain and tip them into a blender with all the other ingredients. Blend until you have a super-smooth, creamy mixture.

Scrape the mixture into a saucepan. Using a spatula, stir the mixture over a low heat until it starts to thicken. Continue to stir until the mixture is really thick and has a melted cheese-like consistency.

It's essential that you stir continuously as it can easily catch on the bottom, which totally spoils the flavour, so try not to have any distractions.

Remove the pan from the heat, pour the "cheese" into your prepared containers and chill in the fridge for 2 hours, or until set through. This "cheese" will keep for 4–5 days in the fridge.

To serve, remove the "cheese" from the container, sprinkle over some additional dried dill and lemon zest, slice and enjoy!

Mushroom pâté
Makes 6–8 servings

360ml (1½ cups) vegan-friendly white wine
30g (1oz) dried mushrooms (such as porcini, shiitake)
3 tbsp coconut oil
2 banana shallots, finely sliced
3 garlic cloves, crushed
2 tbsp fresh thyme leaves
3 portobello mushrooms, diced
500g (1lb 2oz) chestnut (cremini) mushrooms, brushed clean and diced
1 tsp miso paste
½ tsp smoked (or regular) sea salt
1 tsp cracked black pepper
120ml (½ cup) soy or oat cream

Heat the wine gently in a saucepan until just simmering. Put the dried mushrooms in a heatproof bowl, pour over the wine, and let the mushrooms rehydrate for 10 minutes.

Melt the coconut oil in a large, non-stick saucepan over a medium heat. Add the shallots, garlic and thyme. Sauté for 3–4 minutes, stirring, until softened and lightly browned. Add the fresh mushrooms and cook, stirring often, for 5 minutes (they will shrink dramatically as they cook). Cover with a lid in between stirring.

Scoop the rehydrated mushrooms out of the wine and add them to the pan. Pour the wine through a fine sieve into the saucepan to get rid of any grit left behind. Use a wooden spoon to scrape any bits off the bottom of the pan – you want all that flavour. Add the miso paste and seasoning, stir, then let all the mushrooms cook for 10 minutes over a low heat, uncovered, so the liquids evaporate.

Remove from the heat, leave to cool to room temperature, then tip into a blender with the cream. Blitz until smooth. Keep in sterilized jars (see page 114) in the fridge for up to 5 days.

Edible Gifts

Apple and Pear Chutney

I love this chutney – and it stores well, so can easily be
enjoyed in the New Year.

3 tbsp olive oil
1 onion, finely chopped
2 celery sticks, finely chopped
4 garlic cloves, finely chopped
1 red chilli, finely chopped
2 tsp sea salt
1 tsp fennel seeds
1 tsp cumin seeds
1 tsp ground coriander
1 tsp celery salt
3 tbsp tomato purée (paste)
1 tbsp miso paste
1 tbsp fresh thyme leaves,
    finely chopped
1 tbsp fresh sage leaves,
    finely chopped
3 apples, peeled, cored
    and finely diced
2 pears, peeled, cored
    and finely diced
60g (heaped ¼ cup) unrefined
    cane sugar
125ml (½ cup) white wine
    vinegar
2 bay leaves
1 star anise
2 cloves

Makes
2 jars

Cooks In
60 minutes

Difficulty
3/10

GF

Heat the oil in a large saucepan, add the chopped onion, celery, garlic, chilli and salt and sauté until golden and caramelized. Add the spices and let them toast for a minute before stirring through the celery salt, tomato purée and miso paste.

Add the thyme and sage, followed by the apples and pears and stir well. Cook the mix for a few minutes before adding the sugar, vinegar, bay leaves, star anise and cloves. Turn the heat down to low, pop a lid on the saucepan and cook the chutney for 30 minutes, or until thickened and sticky.

When cooked, transfer it to sterilized jars (see page 114) and seal while still hot. The chutney should store for up to 6 weeks.

Brussels Sprout Kimchi

This is the perfect way to liven up and preserve a winter harvest of sprouts. They are a low-cost ingredient in winter, so you can make big batches of your own Brussels sprout kimchi to give away to friends and family.

450g (1lb) Brussels sprouts, halved
5 garlic cloves, minced
2 tbsp minced ginger
5 spring onions (scallions), finely chopped
2 tbsp soy sauce
3 tbsp Korean red chilli flakes (gochugaru)
3 tbsp maple syrup
1 apple, grated
3 tbsp nori powder (optional)
10g (⅓oz) fine sea salt

Makes
1 large jar

Cooks In
45 minutes

Difficulty
5/10

GF

Add all the ingredients to a mixing bowl, then use your hands to massage everything together for 5 minutes (you may want to use gloves). Cover the bowl and set the mixture aside for at least 2 hours.

Place the kimchi into clean glass jars, compacting everything as much as you can. Place a layer of baking paper or cling film (plastic wrap) directly over the top, then seal your jars.

Let the kimchi ferment for 2–5 days out of the fridge (depending on the amount of tang you like), before refrigerating. The kimchi should store for 4–5 weeks in the fridge.

Red Cabbage Sauerkraut

The kraut makes a great gift and is a great way of transforming humble cabbage into a probiotic-rich accompaniment.

1 medium red cabbage
1 apple, grated
1 tsp cracked black pepper
2 tsp caraway seeds
1 tsp coriander seeds
sea salt

Makes
1 large jar

Cooks In
**3 hours +
fermenting time**

Difficulty
3/10

GF

Remove the outer cabbage leaves and set them aside. Cut the cabbage in half and shred it very finely, either with a knife or mandoline.

Add the cabbage to a mixing bowl along with the grated apple, black pepper and caraway and coriander seeds. Mix well, then transfer to your weighing scales.

After measuring the weight of the mix (deducting the weight of the bowl), work out what 3% of that weight is (I always ask siri). Add that weight in sea salt to the mixture – for example, if the total weight of the ingredients is 300g then 3% would work out as 10g, so you'd add 10g of sea salt to the mixture.

Massage the salt into the cabbage mix really firmly for at least 10 minutes – this will break down the cell walls of the cabbage, helping it to release the all-important brine.

Cover over the bowl and set it aside for 2 hours for all the liquid to be drawn out. Meanwhile give some glass jars or your fermentation vessel a really good clean.

After the 2 hours, you should have a lot of liquid. Transfer the cabbage to your clean jars leaving a 2.5cm (1in) gap at the top of the jar. Make sure you've added enough brine to cover the cabbage completely.

Place the reserved cabbage leaves over the top to seal in the cabbage, then use a weight to weigh everything down. Specialist fermentation vessels come with weights, but you can also use things like clean pebbles or a sandwich bag filled with a little water.

Seal the jars and leave them out of the fridge to ferment for up to 14 days. The speed of fermentation all depends on the temperature in your house; the warmer it is, the faster it will ferment. Every day, open the jar to let out any gas that may have built up. You can assess the level of fermentation by tasting the brine. The tangier it is, the more fermented your kraut is. Once you've reached your desired level of tang, remove the weights and cabbage leaves, then place the jars in the fridge where they can store for many months.

Occasionally, check the sauerkraut for any signs of mould on the surface. If you see any mould, skim it off immediately. The sauerkraut underneath should still be fine – mould only usually occurs when not everything is submerged in the brine.

Christmas Cookies

Light, crunchy cookies... perfect to give away as gifts.

125g (½ cup) plant butter
60g (½ cup) icing
    (confectioner's) sugar,
    plus extra for dusting
60g (⅓ cup) light brown sugar
1 tsp vanilla bean paste
275g (generous 2 cups) plain
    (all-purpose) flour, plus extra
    for dusting
½ tsp baking powder
½ tsp bicarbonate of soda

Makes
12–14

Cooks In
45 minutes

Difficulty
5/10

**Can be GF, if GF
flour is used**

Beat together the plant butter, both sugars and the vanilla paste with a wooden spoon in a large mixing bowl until creamy. Sift in the flour and raising agents and bring together until it forms a ball of dough. Lightly knead the dough for a couple of minutes, then wrap it in cling film (plastic wrap) and chill in the fridge for at least an hour.

Preheat the oven to 170°C (340°F) and line a large baking tray with greaseproof paper.

Lightly flour your work surface and rolling pin and roll out the dough to around 4mm (⅛in) thick. Use festive cookie cutters to cut the dough, placing the raw cookies onto the lined baking tray as you go. Bake for 12–15 minutes or until lightly golden. Remove from the oven and let the cookies cool slightly on the tray before carefully transferring them to a wire rack to cool completely.

When the cookies are cool, dust with icing sugar.

Photograph on page 181.

Healthy Chocolate Rocky Road

Chocolatey goodness, these are filled with nuts and dried fruit.
Another amazing stocking filler.

220g (1 cup) raw cacao butter, chopped

125g (1 cup) raw cacao powder

175g (½ cup) maple syrup or agave nectar

1 tsp vanilla bean paste

or use 2 x 100g (3½oz) bars dairy-free dark chocolate

For the toppings

160g (1 cup) chopped dried fruit (pineapple, apricot, banana, cranberries, mango)

150g (1 cup) mixed nuts

40g (½ cup) coconut flakes

Serves
12

Cooks In
30 minutes

Difficulty
2/10

GF

Line a baking tray with greaseproof paper.

Melt the chopped cacao butter in a heatproof mixing bowl set over a small saucepan of simmering water, then lift the bowl off the saucepan.

Whisk in the cacao powder until fully incorporated. Stir in the maple syrup and vanilla bean paste. Give it a quick taste to see if it's sweet enough (add a little more syrup if not), then quickly pour the chocolate onto your lined baking tray.

Alternatively, melt the bars of dairy-free dark chocolate.

Before it sets, sprinkle over the chopped dried fruit, nuts and coconut flakes.

Transfer the rocky road to the fridge to set for at least 3 hours. Break into shards before wrapping in paper and giving it to your loved ones. Don't forget to tell them to keep it in the fridge.

Photograph on page 181.

EDIBLE GIFTS

Coconut Bounties

I love chocolate-covered coconut bars, and they are so simple to veganize. They are light, refreshing and another perfect edible gift idea!

For the filling
180g (2 cups) desiccated coconut
160ml (5½fl oz) coconut cream
125g (½ cup) coconut oil
4 tbsp coconut honey or
    maple syrup
1 tsp vanilla bean paste

For the coating
2 x 100g (3½oz) bars dairy-free
    chocolate, chopped

Makes
8 large bars

Cooks In
**30 minutes +
setting time**

Difficulty
5/10

GF

Line a 23cm (9in) square, loose-bottomed cake tin with greaseproof paper.

Put all the filling ingredients in your blender and whizz until all the ingredients are well incorporated. Tip the mixture into the lined cake tin and push it into the corners. Press the mixture down with the back of a wooden spoon until it's level, then pop the cake tin into your freezer to set while you melt the chocolate.

Melt the chopped chocolate in a heatproof mixing bowl set over a small saucepan of simmering water. When all the chocolate has melted, lift the bowl off the pan and set aside to cool slightly.

Take the chilled filling out of the freezer and slice the coconut into eight bars. Warm your knife under hot water before slicing each time to make this easier.

Line a baking sheet with greaseproof paper. Use a fork to dip the coconut pieces individually in the chocolate, shake off any excess chocolate and place them on the lined tray. Once you've coated all the pieces, pop them in the fridge to set for 2 hours.

Jaffa
Cakes

Vegan jaffa cakes – who would have thought it! The wonders of agar agar. These are very simple to make. Give any vegan these wrapped up in a box and you will make their Christmas.

For the sponge layer
coconut oil, for greasing
120ml (½ cup) soy milk
55g (¼ cup) plant butter
1 tsp orange essence
120g (1 cup) plain (all-purpose) flour
100g (½ cup) unrefined caster
    (superfine) sugar
1 tsp baking powder
¼ tsp fine sea salt
¼ tsp ground cinnamon
¼ tsp ground nutmeg

For the orange jelly
2 tbsp agar agar flakes
120ml (½ cup) cold water
240ml (1 cup) freshly squeezed orange juice
2 tbsp caster (superfine) sugar

For the chocolate topping
2 x 100g (3½oz) bars dairy-free chocolate,
    finely chopped
pinch of sea salt

Makes
24

Cooks In
60 minutes

Difficulty
7/10

**Can be GF, if GF
flour is used**

Make the jelly first as it needs 2 hours to set. Line a baking tray with cling film (plastic wrap). Heat the agar agar and water in a saucepan over a medium heat. Bring to the boil, whisk until the flakes disappear, remove from the heat and add the orange juice and sugar. Whisk until combined, pour onto your lined baking tray and place in the fridge until set.

Preheat the oven to 180°C (360°F). Grease two non-stick muffin trays with coconut oil.

Put the soy milk, plant butter and orange essence into a saucepan and set over a low heat until the spread has melted and everything has mixed together. Combine the flour, sugar, baking powder, salt and spices in a mixing bowl. Make a well in the middle and pour in the orange-milk mixture. Stir well until you have a thick batter.

Spoon a couple of tablespoons of the batter into each hole in your greased tray. Smooth the mixture level, then bake for 8 minutes until lightly golden. Allow to cool slightly in the trays before transferring to a wire rack to cool completely.

Put the chocolate into a heatproof bowl set over a saucepan of simmering water. When melted, lift the bowl off the pan, allow the chocolate to cool slightly, then stir in the salt. Remove the set jelly from the fridge and use a round cutter (just smaller than the cake bases) to cut the jelly. Lift the rounds onto the top of each cake base, then spoon over the chocolate. Spread the coated jaffa cakes out on a plate and allow to set completely in the fridge. It should take about 1 hour. They will keep for 2–3 days in the fridge.

Gaz's Boozy Mince Pies

There's something extra-Christmassy and special about making your own mince pies from scratch. So get those Christmas tunes playing and have a fun time making these.

For the filling
300g (scant 2 cups) mixed dried fruit
2 eating apples (such as Braeburn), grated
juice and zest of 1 orange
juice and zest of ½ lemon
120ml (½ cup) agave nectar
1 tsp allspice
60ml (¼ cup) vegan-friendly brandy

For the pastry
1 quantity of sweet pastry (page 155), or shop-bought short-crust pastry
caster (superfine) sugar, for sprinkling

Makes
24

Cooks In
60 minutes

Difficulty
7/10

Can be GF, if GF flour is used

Thoroughly combine all the filling ingredients in a large mixing bowl. Cover the bowl and leave the mixture overnight, or for at least 12 hours, stirring every now and then, if possible. Spoon the mince pie filling into sterilized jars (page 114) – it will keep for 2 months in the fridge.

When you're ready to make the mince pies, grease a non-stick bun tin and preheat the oven to 180°C (350°F). Sprinkle a little flour onto your work surface and roll out the pastry to around 3mm (⅛in) thick.

Cut 12 circles to fit your bun tray, line the holes and pop a teaspoonful of pie filling mixture into each one. Cut out the tops for each one – in shapes if you wish – and place over the filling, pressing the edges gently to seal. Sprinkle over some caster sugar and bake for 12–15 minutes, or until golden.

Let the mince pies cool before serving with my Mulled wine (page 187) or packaging up to give to friends and family.

Mulled Wine

You can easily make this into mulled cider instead. Just use two 500ml (17fl oz) bottles of vegan cider instead of the red wine.

1 x 75cl bottle vegan red wine
juice and peel of 2 clementines
1 vanilla pod, seeds scraped out
50g (¼ cup) caster (superfine) sugar
4 cloves
2 cinnamon sticks
1 tsp grated nutmeg
1 bay leaf
2 star anise

Serves
4

Cooks In
20 minutes

Difficulty
2/10

GF

Pour half the bottle of wine into a large saucepan. Squeeze in the juice of the clementines and add the peel (it adds great flavour). Add the vanilla pod and seeds followed by the cloves, cinnamon, nutmeg, bay leaf and star anise.

Place the saucepan over a medium heat and bring it to a simmer. Simmer for 10 minutes to let all the flavours infuse. After 10 minutes, pour in the rest of the wine and turn the heat down low. Once piping hot, serve in your favourite Christmas mugs or in heatproof glasses.

Photograph on page 185.

Index

Acknowledgements

Huge thank you for purchasing *Plants Only Holidays*, it was a joy to re-vamp the original Christmas cookbook I made many years ago, adding new, exciting recipes and refreshing the look of the book.

I'd like to thank everyone at Quadrille for all of their help making this happen, and their constant votes of confidence and support in me. Special shout-out to Emily & Stacey for bearing with me and helping me out no end! Also my long-time collaborators White Sky Creative, for helping with the new designs!

Thank you to Simon Smith as always for being a great friend to me and taking lovely photos of my food.

I'd like to thank my Dad, Doug, & lovely friend Elly, for helping me prepare all the dishes at the food shoot.

The lifestyle shoot was so fun at Little Mill Cottage in Wales, with my great friend and colleague Tom shooting the photos – thanks to my incredible Mum, Dad & friends Harlem, Bruna & Shelli for coming along and enjoying the early Christmas dinner with me!

To my lovely agents Zoe & Olivia, thank you for all you do for me!

Mum, I really appreciate all your hard work posting out the books, and keeping things going behind the scenes – I couldn't do what I do without you taking the pressure off my shoulders!

Mum, Dad & my sister, Charlotte, I love you all so much, thanks for being my #1 supporters, always.

Gaz Oakley

MANAGING DIRECTOR Sarah Lavelle

COMMISSIONING EDITOR Stacey Cleworth

COPY EDITOR Samantha Stanley, Rebecca Woods

PROOFREADER Sarah Epton

DESIGNER Joshua Cotterill at White Sky Creative

ASSISTING DESIGNERS Emily Lapworth & Alicia House

PHOTOGRAPHERS Simon Smith, Tom Kong

PROP STYLING Luis Peral, Milly Bruce & Gaz Oakley

FOOD STYLING Gaz Oakley

FOOD STYLING ASSISTANT Joe Horner, Elly Smart & Doug Oakley

PRODUCTION CONTROLLER Nikolaus Ginelli, Martina Georgieva

HEAD OF PRODUCTION Stephen Lang

Content originally taken from
Vegan Christmas (2018)
978 1 78713 267 2

Published in 2024 by Quadrille Publishing Limited

Quadrille
52–54 Southwark Street
London SE1 1UN
quadrille.com

Cataloguing in Publication Data: a catalogue record
for this book is available from the British Library.

Text © Quadrille 2024
Food photography © Simon Smith 2018 & 2024,
except for pages 1, 2, 5, 6, 8, 10, 22, 25, 26, 56, 85,
88, 95, 120, 130, 140, 143, 157, 171, 172, 186
© Tom Kong 2024
Design © Quadrille 2024
Front cover image © Tom Kong 2024

ISBN 978 1 83783 148 7

Printed in China using soy inks